PLANT-BASED COOKBOOK

Quick and easy recipes

Author

Marilyn P. Barrios

Contents

INTRODUCTION

Every now and then, you feel the need to give a twist to a traditional recipe. Sometimes you add a spice or you use a different vegetable and you change the dish completely. Other times, you take out only one ingredient and the whole dinner ends up in the bin.

With a spiralizer, you can still hold on to your adventurous side without altering the ingredients of a dish. Instead, you add flavor to its looks and with only a few twists and turns you give it an eye-catching, stylish presentation that is bound to impress your guests.

The artistic aspect of your plate is not the most important thing, however. The nutritional value is equally crucial. With the spiralizer and the recipes in this book, you will be more inclined to prepare healthy meals and include more fruits and vegetables in your diet.

The Spiralizer in a nutshell

A Spiralizer is a terrific kitchen gadget that will forever change the way you prepare your everyday meals. Long gone are the days when eating a bowl full of pasta left you feeling guilty and worried about your weight.

This awesome tool will allow you to eat pasta for every meal you have and stay lean and fit. The catch is that you will hardly ever consume whole-grain pasta. Instead, you will take forkfuls of noodles made from zucchini, cucumbers, sweet potatoes, beets and apples.

By using the spi3ralizer, you make a choice for a healthier lifestyle by replacing high-carb foods with fresh produce in your diet. With its help, you can transform every hard-textured vegetable or fruit into noodles, shoestrings or spirals that will go perfectly with your dish, whether it is a salad or a soup.

Types of Spiralizers

The spiralizer comes in two versions: the hand-crank model and the hourglass model. Each of them has different characteristics, yet they produce almost the same result. Here are just a few tips that will help you decide which one to choose before ordering one:

- The hand-crank version is the largest one, and it might take a generous amount of space on your countertop. The hourglass model, however, is a smaller, hand-held version of that slicer.
- The bigger spiralizer cuts the produce into various widths, giving you the ultimate experience of spiralizing hard-textured fruits and vegetables. Instead, the hourglass

version might surprise you every now and then with a shred-like pasta that fails to meet the expectations.

- The smaller model is available for prices usually under $40. On the other hand, for the hand-crank version you should pay somewhere between $50 and $100.

How does it work?

The spiralizer is easy to use and once you understand how every fruit or vegetable can be shaped, you will have no trouble in using it again and again. With the hourglass model, you will be able to spiralize your favorite produce in no time. All you should do is to insert it into the holder and slowly push it forward, while twisting it at the same time. The noodles or ribbons will soon come out at the other end.

The hand-crank spiralizer will require a little bit of extra work, but the result will be totally worth it. First you must make sure that your vegetables are washed and their ends are trimmed. Once the tool is set up on your table or countertop, you take the produce and place it on the holder in such a way that it is even with the blade. Next, you activate the crank and the spiralizer will do the job for you by rotating and slicing it into the desired shape.

What can be spiralized?

After preparing just a few recipes with the aid of the spiralizer, you will fall in love with it and you will want to slice and noodle every bit of food in your fridge. However, you must keep in mind that despite being a wonderful tool, the spiralizer will not work with every produce you have on hand. Some fruits or vegetables that contain too much water will only become a mushy paste once you try to slice them this way.

You will get the best results with vegetables like sweet potatoes, zucchini, cucumbers, carrots, turnips or beets. The cabbage can be transformed into appetizing spirals if you take out the core first. Sturdy fruits like apples and even fresh quinces can be spiralized with both versions of the slicer.

What you should avoid spiralizing

At the opposite end of the produce alternatives you will find soft fruits like pears, bananas, avocados, peaches or mangos. Should you attempt to slice any of these, you will end up splashing the entire pulp on your table and you will be looking at a full hour of cleaning the kitchen walls. The same goes for eggplants, tomatoes, watermelons or cantaloupes.

Low carb?

If you are interested in low carb recipes, please look at the nutritional information closely. Although I tried to put as many low carb recipes as possible, there were too many delicious recipes that I couldn't leave out

Tips and Tricks

- Before using the hand-crank spiralizer, place it on a solid, smooth countertop or on the kitchen table.
- Place a bowl or a plate at the other end of the spiralizer. This way, you will avoid spilling the noodles on the table.
- After you finished spiralizing your vegetables, you can use a knife to trim them to your desired length.
- If you have any decaying produce lying around, cut the rotten bits and spiralize the remaining parts. This is a great way to save some of the leftover food from the holidays.
- Measure the thickness of your vegetables before slicing them. If they are larger than the holder, cut them to an appropriate fitting.
- After you spiralize the produce, pat them dry with a kitchen towel. This will take out the excess water and prevent your meal from becoming too moist.
- If you plan to add the resulted noodles to a hot sauce or soup, wait until you have taken the skillet away from the heat. This will maintain the texture of the slices while setting up the plate.

This book contains chapters dedicated to various types of meals that can be prepared with spiralized vegetables or fruits. You won't have to prepare too many recipes before realizing just how better your meals will look and taste.

We have also included nutritional values to each recipe, per serving and based on a 2000 calorie diet (daily intake), so you can pick the ones that best fit your current nutrition plan. With that in mind, we strongly recommend that you try to cook as many recipes as possible to improve your cooking skills and to make the best out of your spiralizer.

Take this book as a source of inspiration for your next low-calorie meal and make cooking more fun. Enjoy!

Trying to be healthy is hard and sometimes confusing. For years we were told that fats were bad for us and we had to cut them out of our diets. Yet we became more obese than any other time in history! But over time science and our understanding of nutrition has improved. We now know that it is actually simple carbs such as sugar and pastas that are making us fat and unhealthy.

By removing simple carbs with healthy fats and protein, the low carb diet forces your body to become a fat burning machine! As a result, you will automatically lose weight, increase your mental focus and decrease your appetite. This book is designed to empower you by providing quick and easy one-skillet recipes that can be made in less time than a TV episode!

With Low Carb in 20 Minutes, you will get...

◆ Over 60 Easy and Delicious Low Carb Recipes for All Meals - Breakfast, Lunch, Dinner, and Snacks!

◆ Full Nutritional Information for Each Recipe Cooking and Preparation Times to Find the Quickest and Easiest Recipes to Make

◆ A Straight Forward Explanation about the Low Carb Diet

◆ The Benefits Of One Skillet Cooking For A Low Carb Diet

To get these delicious recipes and more visit https://www.amazon.com/dp/B01KCS88N0

Are you looking for delicious easy to make low carb slow cooker recipes that the whole family can enjoy? Do you want to be able to make healthy low carb meals but don't want to spend all day in the kitchen?

Trying to be healthy is hard and sometimes confusing. For years we were told that fats were bad for us and we had to cut them out of our diets. Yet we became more obese than any other time in history! But over time science and our understanding of nutrition has improved. We now know that it is actually simple carbs such as sugar and pastas that are making us fat and unhealthy.

By removing simple carbs with healthy fats and protein, the low carb diet forces your body to become a fat burning machine! As a result, you will automatically lose weight, increase your mental focus and decrease your appetite. This book is designed to empower you by providing quick and easy one-skillet recipes that can be made in less time than a TV episode!

With Low Carb Slow Cooker, you will get...

- Over 100 Easy and Delicious Low Carb Recipes for All Meals - Breakfast, Lunch, Dinner, and Snacks!
- Full Nutritional Information for Each Recipe Cooking and Preparation Times to Find the Quickest and Easiest Recipes to Make
- A Straight Forward Explanation about the Low Carb Diet
- The Benefits Of One Slow Cooker and Slow Cooking Tips

BREAKFAST

Bacon, Eggs, And Arugula Parsnip Nests

Prep Time: 5 minutes / Cook Time: 40 minutes

Serves: 8

Preferred spiralizer: Hourglass

Vegetarian-friendly

Good points: This recipe is phosphorus, riboflavin, and selenium

Nutritional Information Per Serving: Calories: 92;

Total Fat: 5 g; Saturated Fat: 1 g; Trans Fat: 0g;

Cholesterol: 160 mg; Sodium: 93 mg; Potassium: 208 mg;

Total Carbs: 7 g; Dietary Fiber: 2 g; Sugar: 2 g;

Protein: 6 g; Vitamin A: 11%; Calcium: 4%;

Vitamin C: 11%; Iron: 5%

Ingredients:

- 2 parsnips, large-sized, peeled, and spiralized using the Blade D, and noodles trimmed into shorter strands
- 2 eggs, beaten
- 1/2 teaspoon garlic powder
- 1 cup baby arugula
- 2 strips bacon
- 8 whole eggs
- Hot sauce, to drizzle
- Salt and pepper, to taste

Directions:

1. Preheat the oven to 425F. Grease a large-sized muffin with nonstick cooking spray.
2. Heat a large-sized skillet over medium-high heat. When hot, add the bacon and cook for about 10 minutes or until cooked and crispy. Transfer into a plate lined with paper towel and let cool. When cool, crumble into small bits.
3. Remove bacon fat from the skillet, leaving 1 tablespoon of the bacon grease. Add the parsnip noodles. Season with salt, garlic powder, and pepper, and toss. Cook for about 5-7 minutes or until cooked through. Transfer into a medium-sized mixing bowl. Let cool for 2 minutes.
4. Add the beaten eggs into the bowl with parsnip noodles and toss to thoroughly coat and combine. Divide and pack the parsnip noodles into muffin cups, creating a well in the center of each. Cook in the oven for 15 minutes.
5. After 15 minutes, remove from the oven and crack an egg into each of the well in the parsnip muffin. Return into the oven and bake for 9 to 12 more or until the eggs are set. After 9 minutes of baking, open the oven and check – shake the muffin pan and if the eggs are still not set, bake for 2 minutes more, and check again.
6. When the eggs are set, remove the muffin pan from the oven and immediately top with the arugula, sprinkle with the bacon crumbs, and dash with hot sauce.

Feta and Butternut Squash Frittata

Prep Time: 10 minutes / Cook Time: 20 minutes

Serves: 4

Preferred spiralizer: Hourglass

Vegetarian-friendly

Good points: This recipe is high in phosphorus, riboflavin, selenium, vitamin A, and vitamin C.

Nutritional Information Per Serving: Calories: 236;

Total Fat: 16g; Saturated Fat: 5g; Trans Fat: 0g;

Cholesterol: 431mg; Sodium: 242mg; Potassium: 270mg;

Total Carbs: 9g; Dietary Fiber: 1g; Sugar: 2g;

Protein: 15 g; Vitamin A: 191%; Calcium: 16%;

Vitamin C: 79%; Iron: 15%

Ingredients:

- 4 eggs, large-sized, beaten
- 1.5 cup butternut squash, spiralized using the Blade D noodles
- 1 packed cup curly kale, chopped
- 2 tablespoons feta cheese, well-crumbled (OR goat cheese OR omit if dairy-free)
- 1/4 teaspoon red pepper flakes
- 1/4 teaspoon paprika
- 1/2 tablespoon extra-virgin olive oil
- 1 garlic clove, small-sized, minced
- Salt and pepper, to taste

Directions:

1. Preheat oven to 425F.
2. Heat a large-sized skillet over medium-high. Add the olive oil. When the oil is hot, add the garlic, kale, and red peppers, and season with salt and pepper. Cook for about 5 minutes or until the kale is mostly wilted. Transfer into an 8-inch oven-safe skillet.
3. In the skillet where you cooked the kale, add the squash noodles. Toss and cook for about 5 minutes or until mostly wilted. Transfer the noodles into the 8-inch skillet.
4. Stir the crumbled feta in the bowl of beaten eggs. Pour the egg mix evenly over the kale and squash noodles in the 8-inch skillet. Season with salt and pepper and cook in the stove top for about 1 minutes or until the bottom of the eggs are set.
5. Bake the 8-inch skillet in the oven for about 10 to 13 minutes or until the eggs are cooked through and the edges are lightly browned and a toothpick comes out when inserted with a toothpick. Remove from the oven. Divide into 4 slices and serve.

Zucchini Noodles and Green Pepper Frittata

Prep Time: 10 minutes / Cook Time: 40 minutes

Serves: 4

Preferred spiralizer: Hourglass

Vegetarian-friendly

Good points: This recipe is very high in vitamin C and selenium, and low in sugar

Nutritional Information Per Serving: Calories: 571;

Total Fat: 47.1g; Saturated Fat: 24.6g; Trans Fat: 0g;

Cholesterol: 467mg; Sodium: 719mg; Potassium: 602mg;

Total Carbs: 9.7g; Dietary Fiber: 1.2g; Sugar: 3.5g;

Protein: 29.1g; Vitamin A 52%; Calcium: 37%;

Vitamin C: 110%; Iron: 16%

Ingredients

- 8 large eggs, beaten
- ½ cup arrowroot flour or tapioca flour
- 1 teaspoon of baking powder
- 1 cup of green bell peppers, diced
- 1 zucchini, spiralized
- 1 cup of cottage cheese
- 1 cup of Cheddar cheese, grated
- ½ cup of melted butter
- 1 tablespoon of canola oil
- Salt and pepper to taste

Directions:

1. Preheat the oven to 400 degrees Fahrenheit.
2. In a large bowl, mix the dry ingredients: flour, baking powder, salt and pepper.
3. In another bowl, combine the eggs with the butter, the cottage cheese and the Cheddar cheese.
4. Add the second mixture to the first and pour in the diced bell peppers and zucchini noodles, too. Mix well.
5. Coat a baking tray with the canola oil and pour this mixture in.
6. Place the tray into the oven and cook for 15 minutes, before lowering the heat to 325 degrees Fahrenheit. Cook for another 35 minutes.
7. Remove the tray from the oven and let it cool down for a few minutes before cutting slices and transferring them to the serving dishes.

Breakfast Eggs and Zoodles

Prep Time: 5 minutes / Cook Time: 5 minutes

Serves: 1

Preferred spiralizer: Hourglass

Vegetarian-friendly

Good points: This recipe is high in riboflavin, selenium, and vitamin C

Nutritional Information Per Serving: Calories: 275;

Total Fat: 22.7g; Saturated Fat: 14.6g; Trans Fat: 0g;

Cholesterol: 327mg; Sodium: 298mg; Potassium: 633mg;

Total Carbs: 7.3g; Dietary Fiber: 2.2g; Sugar: 4.1g;

Protein: 13.5g; Vitamin A: 16%; Calcium: 8%;

Vitamin C: 56%; Iron: 13%

Ingredients:

- 2 eggs
- 1 zucchini, small-sized, spiralized
- 1 tablespoon coconut oil
- pepper
- salt
- seasonings

Directions:

1. Put the coconut oil in a frying pan and melt over medium heat. When the oil is heated, add the zoodles and sauté for a few minutes. Crack the eggs on top of the zoodle and cover the pan with lid. Check that the zoodles are not burning – they contain plenty of water, but if your zoodles are dry, add a splash of water in the pan to prevent them from burning.
2. Cook for about 4 minutes or until the egg whites are set, but the yolks are still soft. If desired, cook longer until the eggs reach your desired doneness, making sure the zoodles are not burnt.
3. Season to taste with salt, pepper, and your favor seasoning, such as parsley or basil. Serve and enjoy!

Cheesy Zoodle Breakfast Nests

Prep Time: 10 minutes / Cook Time: 15 minutes

Serves: 4

Preferred spiralizer: Hourglass

Vegetarian-friendly

Good points: This recipe is very high in vitamin c and high in vitamin B6, vitamin A, selenium, riboflavin, and phosphorus

Nutritional Information Per Serving: Calories: 128;

Total Fat: 5.6g; Saturated Fat: 2.2g; Trans Fat: 0g;

Cholesterol: 128mg; Sodium: 232mg; Potassium: 393mg;

Total Carbs: 11.5g; Dietary Fiber: 1.9; Sugar: 3.3g;

Protein: 9.2g; Vitamin A: 14%; Calcium: 12%;

Vitamin C: 35%; Iron: 8%

Ingredients:

- 3 eggs, beaten

- 2 zucchinis, spiralized
- 1/3 cup panko breadcrumbs
- 1/3 cup fresh grated Parmesan
- 1 tomato, seed and diced
- 3 fresh basil leaves, chopped
- Salt and pepper, to taste
- Nonstick cooking spray, for greasing the cupcake/muffin tins

Directions:

1. Preheat the oven to 375F.
2. In a medium-sized mixing bowl, mix all the ingredients together. If your zoodles are too long, then cut them into smaller bite-sized strands.
3. Grease the cupcake/muffin tins with nonstick cooking spray. Spoon the zoodle mixture into each cup, pressing down with the back of the spoon to pack the mix into the cups.
4. If desired, top with extra parmesan cheese.
5. Bake for about 15 minutes and eat while they are still warm.

Spiralized Sriracha Garlic Hash Browns and Baked Eggs

Prep Time: 5 minutes / Cook Time: 5-15 minutes

Serves: 2

Preferred spiralizer: Hourglass

Vegetarian-friendly

Good points: This recipe is very high in vitamin B6 and vitamin C, high in manganese, and has no cholesterol

Nutritional Information Per Serving: Calories: 129;

Total Fat: 7.1g; Saturated Fat: 1g; Trans Fat: 0g;

Cholesterol: 0mg; Sodium: 134mg; Potassium: 305mg;

Total Carbs: 15.6g; Dietary Fiber: 2.1g; Sugar: 3.8g;

Protein: 1.7g; Vitamin A: 4%; Calcium: 2%;

Vitamin C: 35%; Iron: 12%

Ingredients:

- 1 yam, large-sized, peeled and spiralized
- 1 tablespoon extra-virgin olive oil
- 1-2 tablespoons garlic, minced
- 2 teaspoons sriracha, or more to taste
- Salt and pepper, to taste

Directions:

1. Peel the yam and then spiralize using the smallest blade of your spiralizer.
2. With a scissor, cut the yam noodles a couple of times so they are easier to eat.
3. In a large-sized saucepan, put the 1 tablespoon oil and heat over medium heat. Add 1 to 2 tablespoons of minced garlic and sauté for a bit. Add the yam noodles, season with salt and pepper to taste, and add sriracha to taste. Sauté for about 5 to 10 minutes, stirring and tossing continuously or until the yam is cooked through.
4. When the yam noodles are cooked through, continue cooking for 1-2 minutes, pressing down the yam using a spatula to brown. Flip and cook the other side for about 1-2 minutes or until browned.
5. Serve with baked eggs.

Yellow Squash and Egg Breakfast

Prep Time: 5 minutes / Cook Time: 10 minutes

Serves: 1

Preferred spiralizer: Hourglass

Vegetarian-friendly

Good points: This recipe is very high in vitamin C and vitamin B6, and high in phosphorus, potassium, riboflavin, selenium, and vitamin A.

Nutritional Information Per Serving: Calories: 34;

Total Fat: 2.2 g; Saturated Fat: 1g; Trans Fat: 0g;

Cholesterol: 44mg; Sodium: 59mg; Potassium: 147mg;

Total Carbs: 2g; Dietary Fiber: 0.6g; Sugar: 0.9g;

Protein: 2g; Vitamin A: 4%; Calcium: 1%;

Vitamin C: 14%; Iron: 2%

Ingredients

- 1 yellow squash, small-sized
- 1 egg
- 1 garlic clove, small-sized, minced
- 1 teaspoon ghee
- Pepper
- Pinch fresh basil
- Salt

Directions:

1. Spiralize the yellow squash using the flat blade of your spiralizer.
2. Put the ghee in a sauté pan and melt over medium heat. Add the garlic and sauté until fragrant.
3. Add the squash in the pan; toss and cook for a couple of minutes until softened. Transfer the squash into a plate.
4. Crack the egg in the same pan and cook until the egg white is opaque on the bottom. Add a splash of water into the pan and cover with the lid. Cook for 4 minutes or until the egg white is set, but the yolks still runny, or until the eggs are cooked to your preferred doneness.

5. Plate the egg on top of the cooked squash and season to taste with salt and pepper and with a pinch of basil. Serve.

Grated Egg, Caramelized Onions, and Bacon Butternut Squash Rice

Prep Time: 15 minutes / Cook Time: 25 minutes

Serves: 5

Preferred spiralizer: Hourglass

Vegetarian-friendly

Good points: This recipe is high in selenium, vitamin A, and vitamin C.

Nutritional Information Per Serving: Calories: 178;

Total Fat: 9.2g; Saturated Fat: 2.9g; Trans Fat: 0g;

Cholesterol: 115mg; Sodium: 431mg; Potassium: 549mg;

Total Carbs: 14.8g; Dietary Fiber: 2.6g; Sugar: 3.2g;

Protein: 10.5g; Vitamin A: 243%; Calcium: 7%;

Vitamin C: 41%; Iron: 9%

Ingredients:

- 1 butternut squash, large-sized, peeled, and spiralized using Blade D
- 4 slices bacon
- 3 eggs, hard boiled, peeled
- 1/4 teaspoon garlic powder
- 1/4 cup chicken broth, low-sodium
- 1/2 teaspoon paprika
- 1/2 red onion, peeled, and spiralized using Blade A, noodles trimmed
- Salt and pepper

Directions:

1. Put the squash noodles into a food processor and pulse until the consistency is rice-like. Set aside.

2. Heat a large-sized skillet over a medium-high. Add the bacon and cook for 7 minutes, flipping halfway through, until crispy. Transfer to a plate lined with paper towel.
3. Immediately put the onions into the skillet. Season with pepper and salt. Cook for 10 minutes until starting to brown and until caramelized. Transfer to a plate and set aside.
4. Immediately put the butternut squash rice, season with salt, pepper, paprika, and garlic powder. Stir to mix. Pour the chicken broth in the skillet. Cook for about 7 minutes or until the rice is soft.
5. Stir in the crumbled bacon and onions. Cook for about 1 minute or until heated through.
6. Divide the rice mix between 5 bowls. Grate the eggs over each bowl, about 3/4 an egg into each bowl.

Western Vegetarian Omelette

Prep Time: 10 minutes / Cook Time: 10 minutes

Serves: 2

Preferred spiralizer: Hourglass

Vegetarian-friendly

Good points: This recipe is low in sodium, high in selenium, and very high in vitamin A and C.

Nutritional Information Per Serving: Calories: 170;

Total Fat: 11.8g; Saturated Fat: 2.7g; Trans Fat: 0g;

Cholesterol: 164mg; Sodium: 67mg; Potassium: 406mg;

Total Carbs: 10.9g; Dietary Fiber: 3.5g; Sugar: 5.4g;

Protein: 7.2g; Vitamin A: 50%; Calcium: 4%;

Vitamin C: 206%; Iron: 9%

Ingredients:

- 2 eggs, beaten
- 1 green or red bell pepper, spiralized using Blade A and noodles trimmed
- 1/2 yellow or white onion, small-sized, spiralized using Blade A and noodles 1/4 teaspoon dried thyme

- 1/4 avocado, pitted, peeled and then sliced
- 1/3 cup tomatoes, diced (I use Roma tomatoes)
- trimmed
- 1 teaspoon extra-virgin olive oil
- Salt and pepper

To serve:

- Salsa
- Green salad

Directions:

1. Put a 10-inch skillet over medium-high heat. When hot, add the olive oil. When the oil is shimmering, add the onions and bell peppers. Season with salt, pepper, and thyme. Cook for about 5 to 7 minutes or until wilted.
2. Pour the eggs over into the skillet, tilting the pan to fill the bottom of the skillet with the egg.
3. Sprinkle with the tomatoes. Cook for about 2 minutes or until the bottom of the eggs are set. Run a spatula around the edges and then under the omelet to loosen from the skillet. Flip the omelet and cook for 2 minutes more. Fold in half and, using the spatula, press down to tighten the omelet.
4. Transfer into a plate, top with avocado, and, if desired, serve with greens.

Fried Eggs with Zucchini Noodles and Walnuts

Prep Time: 10 minutes / Cook Time: 10 minutes

Serves: 2

Preferred spiralizer: Hourglass

Vegetarian-friendly

Good points: This recipe is high in manganese and selenium, as well as low in sugar and sodium

Nutritional Information Per Serving: Calories: 456;

Total Fat: 39g; Saturated Fat: 6.9g; Trans Fat: 0g;

Cholesterol: 383mg; Sodium: 177mg; Potassium: 510mg;

Total Carbs: 9.3g; Dietary Fiber: 3.5g; Sugar: 3.6g;

Protein: 21.9g; Vitamin A 15%; Calcium: 10%;

Vitamin C: 22%; Iron: 18%.

Ingredients

- 4 large eggs, beaten
- 1 cup of zucchini, spiralized into large noodles
- 1 small onion, diced
- ½ cup of walnuts, crushed
- 1 tablespoon of canola oil
- ¼ teaspoon of chili flakes
- 2 tablespoons of cream cheese
- Salt and pepper, to taste

Directions:

1. Heat the oil in a medium-sized skillet. Add the onion and the zucchini. Season them with salt, pepper and the chili flakes. Cook for 3 minutes.
2. Add the crushed walnuts and mix well. Cook for another 3 minutes.
3. Add the beaten eggs and distribute the mixture evenly across the pan using a wooden spoon.
4. Cook until the eggs are solid.
5. Remove from the heat and divide into the serving dishes. Add a spoonful of cream cheese to each dish and serve right away.

Spiralized Zucchini Bruschetta Omelette

Prep Time: 5 minutes / Cook Time: 10 minutes

Serves: 1

Preferred spiralizer: Hourglass

Vegetarian-friendly

Good points: This recipe is high in phosphorus, riboflavin, vitamin A, and vitamin C, and very high in selenium.

Nutritional Information Per Serving: Calories: 288;

Total Fat: 20.5g; Saturated Fat: 5.2g; Trans Fat: 0g;

Cholesterol: 491mg; Sodium: 200mg; Potassium: 674mg;

Total Carbs: 9.1g; Dietary Fiber: 2.3g; Sugar: 5.2g;

Protein: 18.9g; Vitamin A: 34%; Calcium: 10%;

Vitamin C: 51%; Iron: 18%

Ingredients:

For the omelet:

- 3 eggs, larges-sized, beaten
- 1/2 zucchini, medium-sized, spiralized using Blade D and noodles trimmed
- Salt and pepper, to taste

For the bruschetta:

- 1 garlic clove, minced
- 1/2 cup cherry tomatoes, halved
- 1/2 tablespoon extra-virgin olive oil
- 1/2 tablespoon red wine vinegar
- 5 basil leaves, chopped
- salt and pepper, to taste

Directions:

1. Heat a small-sized skillet over medium-high heat. Coat with nonstick cooking spray. When hot, add the zoodles. Cook for about 3 minutes or until al dente and wilted. When the zoodles are cooked, distribute evenly on the bottom of the skillet.
2. Pour the beaten eggs over and season with pepper and salt. Cook for about 3 minutes or until the bottom sets. Cover and cook for 5 minutes or until the eggs are cooked all the way through.
3. While the egg is cooking, put all the bruschetta ingredients in a medium-sized mixing bowl and toss to combine. Set aside.
4. When the omelet is cooked, transfer into a plate. Top with the bruschetta and immediately serve.

Spiralized Zucchini with Ricotta Dressing

Prep Time: 10 minutes / Cook Time: 15 minutes

Serves: 2

Preferred spiralizer: Hourglass

Gluten-free, Vegetarian-friendly

Good points: This recipe is high in calcium, selenium and vitamin C

Nutritional Information Per Serving: Calories: 335;

Total Fat: 24.5g; Saturated Fat: 8.3g; Trans Fat: 0g;

Cholesterol: 38mg; Sodium: 1195mg; Potassium: 700mg;

Total Carbs: 15.7g; Dietary Fiber: 3.4g; Sugar: 4 g;

Protein: 17.5g; Vitamin A 20%; Calcium: 38%;

Vitamin C: 62%; Iron: 10%

Ingredients

- 2 zucchinis, spiralized
- 1 cup of Ricotta cheese
- 1/2 cup of capers
- 1 garlic clove, minced
- 1 teaspoon of lime juice
- 1 teaspoon of lemon zest
- 2 tablespoons of olive oil
- 1/4 teaspoon of red pepper flakes
- Salt and pepper

Directions:

1. Place a skillet over medium heat. Add a tablespoon of olive oil and once it heats up, add the spiralized zucchinis. Toss and cook for a few minutes, until they become crisp.
2. Sprinkle the red pepper flakes, salt and pepper over, before taking them out. Place the zucchinis on a paper towel lined plate.
3. Use a food processor to mix the Ricotta cheese with the capers, the minced garlic clove, the lime juice and the zest. A chunky dressing should result.

4. Put the zucchinis on a serving plate and add the Ricotta dressing. Serve immediately!

SALADS

Cucumber Noodle Salad with Feta Cheese

Prep Time: 5 minutes / Cook Time: 10 minutes

Serves: 2

Preferred spiralizer: Hourglass

Gluten-free, Vegetarian-friendly

Good points: This recipe is low in sodium

Nutritional Information Per Serving: Calories: 354;

Total Fat: 30.8g; Saturated Fat: 9.1g; Trans Fat: 0g;

Cholesterol: 30mg; Sodium: 184mg; Potassium: 530mg;

Total Carbs: 14.3g; Dietary Fiber: 2.3g; Sugar: 6.5g;

Protein: 9.4g; Vitamin A 13%; Calcium: 27%;

Vitamin C: 23%; Iron: 7%.

Ingredients

- 2 medium-sized cucumbers, spiralized
- 1/2 of red onion, diced
- 1/2 cup crumbled feta cheese
- 3 tablespoons of olive oil
- 2 teaspoons of red wine vinegar
- 1 tablespoon of lemon juice
- 1/2 teaspoon of oregano
- Salt and pepper, to taste

Directions:

1. Into a large salad bowl, mix the cucumber spirals with the diced onion and set aside.
2. In a small bowl, mix the olive oil with the red wine vinegar, the lemon juice and season the dressing with salt, pepper and oregano.
3. Pour the dressing over the cucumber and onion and sprinkle the feta cheese.

4. Serve immediately.

Spiralized Cucumber Solomona Salad

Prep Time: 20 minutes / Cook Time: 0 minutes

Serves: 3-4

Preferred spiralizer: Hourglass

Vegetarian-friendly

Good points: This recipe is high in potassium and vitamin and has no cholesterol

Nutritional Information Per Serving: Calories: 81;

Total Fat: 2.7g; Saturated Fat: 0g; Trans Fat: 0g;

Cholesterol: 0mg; Sodium: 859mg; Potassium: 309mg;

Total Carbs: 14.4g; Dietary Fiber: 1.2g; Sugar: 4.4g;

Protein: 1.7g; Vitamin A: 4%; Calcium: 5%;

Vitamin C: 9%; Iron: 5%

Ingredients:

- 2 English cucumbers
- 1/4 teaspoon soy sauce, reduced sodium
- 1 teaspoon toasted sesame oil
- 1 teaspoon coarse ground kosher salt
- 1 tablespoon granulated sugar, honey, or agave
- 2 teaspoons toasted sesame seeds
- 3 tablespoons seasoned rice vinegar

Directions:

1. Cut the ends of the cucumbers off and spiralizer, following the instructions of your spiralizer's manual.
2. Put the zoodles in a bowl and sprinkle with the kosher salt. Toss to combine and let sit for 10 minutes.

3. Remove the cucumber from the bowl and drain any excess water. Using paper towels, gently dab the cucumber to remove extra water. Transfer into a serving bowl.
4. In a small-sized bowl, combine the sesame oil, soy sauce, rice vinegar, and sugar by lightly whisking.
5. Pour the sesame oil mix over the cucumber and toss to coat.
6. Sprinkle with the sesame seeds and then toss again. Serve immediately.

Spiralized Carrot and Cucumber Salad

Prep Time: 15 minutes / Cook Time: 1 hour

Serves: 6

Preferred spiralizer: Hourglass

Vegetarian-friendly

Good points: This recipe is very high in vitamin A, high in fiber, manganese, potassium, and vitamin C, and has no cholesterol

Nutritional Information Per Serving: Calories: 56;

Total Fat: 2.6g; Saturated Fat: 0g; Trans Fat: 0g;

Cholesterol: 0mg; Sodium: 130mg; Potassium: 237mg;

Total Carbs: 7.3g; Dietary Fiber: 1.6g; Sugar: 3.1g;

Protein: 1g; Vitamin A: 138%; Calcium: 3%;

Vitamin C: 10%; Iron: 3%

Ingredients:

- 1 cucumber
- 4 carrots
- 2 teaspoons soy sauce
- 2 teaspoons ginger, grated
- 2 tablespoons rice wine vinegar
- 2 scallions, chopped
- 1 teaspoon sesame seeds
- 1 tablespoon sesame oil
- 1 lime, juiced

Directions:

1. Peel the cucumber and carrots and then spiralize them into noodles. Put them in a large-sized bowl and toss with the scallions.
2. In a small-sized bowl, whisk the vinegar with the soy sauce, ginger, and lime juice. Pour the mix over the cucumber and the carrots; toss to coat well and sprinkle with the sesame seeds.
3. Cover and refrigerate to chill for at least 1 hour. Serve.

Mediterranean Zoodle Salad

Prep Time: 10 minutes / Cook Time: 10 minutes

Serves: 8

Preferred spiralizer: Hourglass

Vegetarian-friendly

Good points: This recipe is low in cholesterol, high in fiber and vitamin B6, and very high in vitamin C.

Nutritional Information Per Serving: Calories: 132;

Total Fat: 9.5g; Saturated Fat: 2.5g; Trans Fat: 0g;

Cholesterol: 8mg; Sodium: 237mg; Potassium: 467mg;

Total Carbs: 10.2g; Dietary Fiber: 4.3g; Sugar: 2.9g;

Protein: 4.3g; Vitamin A: 9 %; Calcium: 9%;

Vitamin C: 38%; Iron: 8%

Ingredients:

- 3 zucchinis, medium-sized, spiralized
- 1/2 cup feta cheese, crumbled
- 1/2 cup black olives, sliced
- 1 cup cherry tomatoes, halved
- 1 can (15 ounces) artichoke hearts, drained and diced
- Salt and pepper, to taste

For the dressing:

- 1/4 cup sun-dried tomatoes, oil-packed
- 1/4 cup olive oil
- 1 clove garlic
- 2 tablespoons balsamic vinegar
- 2 tablespoons water
- Salt and pepper, to taste

Directions:

1. Put the zoodles, feta, tomatoes, and artichoke hearts in a large-sized bowl, and toss to combine. Season to taste with salt and pepper.
2. Put the garlic, water, vinegar, and sundried tomatoes in a food processor. Process and with the motor running, drizzle the oil through the top, pulsing the dressing until completely smooth. Season to taste with pepper and salt.
3. When ready to serve, toss the zoodle mixture with the dressing.

Spiralized Cucumber Tzatziki Salad

Prep Time: 15 minutes / Cook Time: 0 minutes

Serves: 4

Preferred spiralizer: Hourglass

Vegetarian-friendly

Good points: This recipe is high in calcium, phosphorus, potassium, riboflavin, and vitamin C, and low in cholesterol

Nutritional Information Per Serving: Calories: 82;

Total Fat: 1.7g; Saturated Fat: 1.2g; Trans Fat: 0g;

Cholesterol: 4mg; Sodium: 498mg; Potassium: 361mg;

Total Carbs: 9.4g; Dietary Fiber: 0.9g; Sugar: 5.5g;

Protein: 8.4g; Vitamin A: 4%; Calcium: 14%;

Vitamin C: 11%; Iron: 5%

Ingredients:

- 2 cucumbers

For the tzatziki:

- 10 ounces' Greek yogurt, nonfat
- 2 teaspoons garlic, minced
- 1 tablespoon dill, fresh or dry
- 1 teaspoon sea salt
- 1 squeeze of lemon

Directions:

1. Mix all the tzatziki ingredients together in a bowl until well combined and set aside.
2. Spiralize the cucumber. With scissors, cut the cucumbers into smaller, eatable pieces.
3. Pour the tzatziki sauce over the cucumbers and mix to combine.

Carrot Noodles and Broccoli Salad

Prep Time: 5 minutes / Cook Time: 10 minutes

Serves: 4

Preferred spiralize: Hourglass

Vegetarian-friendly, Gluten-free

Good points: This recipe is high in vitamins A and C and manganese, and it has low cholesterol

Nutritional Information Per Serving: Calories: 112;

Total Fat: 1.8g; Saturated Fat: 1.1g; Trans Fat: 0g;

Cholesterol: 4mg; Sodium: 135mg; Potassium: 495mg;

Total Carbs: 15.7g; Dietary Fiber: 3.4g; Sugar: 8.8g;

Protein: 9.1g; Vitamin A 279%; Calcium: 12%;

Vitamin C: 51%; Iron: 3%

Ingredients

- 3 cups of carrot noodles
- 1 cup of broccoli stems
- 1 red onion, small
- 2 tablespoons of lemon juice
- 1 cup of Greek Yogurt
- 1 tablespoon of Dijon mustard
- ½ teaspoon of garlic powder
- Salt and pepper, to taste

Directions:

1. Spiralize the carrots and set aside.
2. Finely chop the onion and place it in a medium-sized bowl. Add the lemon juice, the yogurt, the Dijon mustard, the garlic powder and mix thoroughly. Sprinkle salt and pepper to taste.
3. In a large bowl, place the carrot noodles and the broccoli stems and pour over the yogurt-based dressing. Serve right away!

Spiralized Zucchini, Avocado, and, Edamame Salad

Prep Time: 20 minutes / Cook Time: 0 minutes

Serves: 4

Preferred spiralizer: Hourglass

Vegetarian-friendly

Good points: This recipe is very high in vitamin C, high in fiber, potassium, thiamin, and has no cholesterol

Nutritional Information Per Serving: Calories: 168;

Total Fat: 12.2g; Saturated Fat: 2.1g; Trans Fat: 0g;

Cholesterol: 0mg; Sodium: 97mg; Potassium: 670mg;

Total Carbs: 10.6g; Dietary Fiber: 4.8g; Sugar: 2g;

Protein: 7.4g; Vitamin A: 7%; Calcium: 10%;

Vitamin C: 59%; Iron: 11%

Ingredients:

- 2 ounces' avocado, diced (1/2 medium-sized)
- 1 zucchini, medium-sized, ends trimmed off
- 1/3 cup cooked edamame, shelled
- 1/2 tablespoon olive oil
- 1/2 lemon
- 1 teaspoon chive, minced
- 1 basil leaf, minced
- Fresh black pepper, to taste
- Kosher salt, to taste

Directions:

1. Spiralize the zucchini into thin spaghetti-like strands.
2. With scissors cut the strands into about 8-inches long, bite-sized lengths and put into a large-sized work bowl.
3. Drizzle with the olive oil, lemon juice, and season to taste with salt and pepper. Toss to combine.
4. Dice the avocado into small-sized pieces. Add to bowl. Add the edamame, chives, and basil, and gently toss and serve right away.

Sweet and Sour Spiralized Salad

Prep Time: 15 minutes / Cook Time: 0 minutes

Serves: 4

Preferred spiralizer: Hourglass

Vegetarian-friendly

Good points: This recipe is very high in vitamin A, vitamin C, and potassium, and high in fiber, manganese, pantothenic acid, phosphorus, thiamin, and vitamin B6, has no cholesterol, and is low in saturated fat.

Nutritional Information Per Serving: Calories: 56;

Total Fat: 0.4g; Saturated Fat: 0g; Trans Fat: 0g;

Cholesterol: 0mg; Sodium: 48mg; Potassium: 520mg;

Total Carbs: 13.7g; Dietary Fiber: 2.7g; Sugar: 6.6g;

Protein: 2.3g; Vitamin A: 15%; Calcium: 5%;

Vitamin C: 29%; Iron: 5%

Ingredients:

- 3 cucumber, large-sized, OR 1 long English cucumber, spiralized
- 2 tablespoons water
- 2 roma tomatoes, chopped
- 10 drops liquid stevia OR 1 packet Stevia granule
- 1/4 fresh lemon juice
- 1 purple onion, spiralized
- croutons, optional
- feta cheese
- pepper
- salt

Directions:

1. In a large-sized serving bowl, put the spiraled cucumbers, tomatoes, and onions.
2. In a small-sized bowl, mix the rest of the ingredients together, except for the croutons.
3. Pour the honey mixture over the vegetables and then toss to coat well.
4. Cover and chill in the refrigerator.
5. Just before serving, top with croutons and feta cheese.

Ranch Spiralized Cucumber Salad

Prep Time: minutes / Cook Time: minutes

Serves: 4

Preferred spiralizer: Hourglass

Vegetarian-friendly

Good points: This recipe is very high in potassium, vitamin C, high in calcium, fiber, iron, manganese, pantothenic acid, phosphorus, and vitamin B6, low in saturated fat, and has no cholesterol

Nutritional Information Per Serving: Calories: 34;

Total Fat: 0.3g; Saturated Fat: 0g; Trans Fat: 0g;

Cholesterol: 0mg; Sodium: 156mg; Potassium: 261mg;

Total Carbs: 7.9g; Dietary Fiber: 1.1g; Sugar: 3.5g;

Protein: 1.5g; Vitamin A: 9%; Calcium: 4%;

Vitamin C: 10%; Iron: 5%

Ingredients:

- 2 cucumbers
- 1/3 cup red onion, cut into strips
- 1/3 cup ranch dressing
- 1 tablespoon dill, finely chopped
- Salt and pepper, to taste

Directions:

1. Spiralize the cucumber into zoodles. Put the zoodles in a bowl and toss with the rest with the ingredients. Store in the fridge until ready to serve.

Cabbage Noodles and Spicy Tuna Salad

Prep Time: 10 minutes / Cook Time: 10 minutes

Serves: 2

Preferred spiralize: Hand-crank

Vegetarian-friendly, Gluten free, Paleo-friendly

Good points: This recipe is high in niacin, selenium, phosphorous and vitamin B12

Nutritional Information Per Serving: Calories: 492;

Total Fat: 28.7g; Saturated Fat: 5g; Trans Fat: 0g;

Cholesterol: 55mg; Sodium: 199mg; Potassium: 804mg;

Total Carbs: 8.5g; Dietary Fiber: 2.6g; Sugar: 3.8g;

Protein: 49.3g; Vitamin A 5%; Calcium: 5%;

Vitamin C: 49%; Iron: 9%.

Ingredients

- 2 cups of cabbage, spiralized into large noodles
- 2 cans of tuna, chunks
- 1 small red onion, diced
- 2 cloves of garlic, minced
- 1 pinch red pepper flakes
- ¼ cup chicken broth
- 2 tablespoons olive oil
- Salt and pepper, to taste

Directions:

1. Use a small saucepan to fry the garlic and red pepper flakes into the olive oil, over medium heat.
2. Add the spiralized cabbage and toss the mixture for a few minutes.
3. Pour in the chicken broth and let it reduce before adding the chunks of tuna.
4. Mix it all together and let it cook for 3 minutes.
5. Serve right away.

Spiralized Courgette Mediterranean Salad

Prep Time: 15 minutes / Cook Time: 0 minutes

Serves: 4

Preferred spiralizer: Hourglass

Vegetarian-friendly

Good points: This recipe is high in vitamin C

Nutritional Information Per Serving: Calories: 226;

Total Fat: 21.6g; Saturated Fat: 6.5g; Trans Fat: 0g;

Cholesterol: 22mg; Sodium: 481mg; Potassium: 396mg;

Total Carbs: 11.3g; Dietary Fiber: 3.4g; Sugar: 5.4g;

Protein: 6.6g; Vitamin A: 15%; Calcium: 17%;

Vitamin C: 48%; Iron: 9%

Ingredients:

- 2 zucchinis, medium-sized
- 2-3 handfuls baby plum tomatoes
- 100 grams' feta cheese
- 2 handfuls Kalamata olives, pitted
- 2 handfuls pine nuts
- 1/2 red onion
- 2 roasted peppers, from a jar
- 2 tablespoons balsamic vinegar
- 3 tablespoons olive oil, extra-virgin
- Salt and pepper
- Small bunch basil

Directions:

2. Spiralize the zucchini into zoodles and put into a salad bowl.
3. Add the tomatoes, olives, roasted pepper, and onion in the bowl.
4. Add the olive oil, balsamic vinegar, and season to taste with salt and pepper.
5. Just before serving, top with the feta cheese, pine nuts, and basil leaves.

Spiralized Beet, Pistachios, and Ricotta Salad

Prep Time: 20 minutes, plus marinating time / Cook Time: 0 minutes

Serves: 4-6

Preferred spiralizer: Hourglass

Vegetarian-friendly

Good points: This recipe is high in vitamin C and has no cholesterol

Nutritional Information Per Serving: Calories: 183;

Total Fat: 14.7g; Saturated Fat: 2g; Trans Fat: 0g;

Cholesterol: 0mg; Sodium: 154mg; Potassium: 419mg;

Total Carbs: 13g; Dietary Fiber: 3g; Sugar: 8.9g;

Protein: 2.9g; Vitamin A: 12%; Calcium: 4%;

Vitamin C: 27%; Iron: 11%

Ingredients:

For the vinaigrette:

- 2 tablespoons orange juice, freshly squeezed
- 1/4 cup olive oil
- 1 teaspoon Dijon mustard
- 1 tablespoon white wine vinegar
- 1 shallot, small-sized, minced
- Kosher salt and freshly ground black pepper, to taste

For the salad:

- 2 red beets, medium-sized, peeled and then spiralized
- 2 ounces' ricotta salata, crumbled
- 2 golden beets, medium-sized, peeled and then spiralized
- 1/4 cup toasted pistachios, roughly chopped
- 1/4 cup parsley leaves
- 1/4 cup mint leaves

Directions:

1. Except for the olive oil, pepper, and salt, whisk the rest of the vinaigrette ingredients in a small-sized bowl. While whisking slowly, add in the olive oil until the mix is smooth and then season with salt and pepper.
2. Put the golden beets in a medium-sized bowl and put the red beets into another medium-sized bowl. Toss each with 1/4 of the dressing and let marinate for at least 30 minutes.
3. Divide the parsley and mint leaves between the bowls. Toss each to combine.
4. Transfer the salads in a platter, layering the golden and red mixtures. Garnish with the pistachios and ricotta salata. Serve.

SNACKS AND SIDES

Raw Zucchini Noodles with Bacon, Goat Cheese and Sweet-Sour Dressing

Prep Time: 10 minutes / Cook Time: 15 minutes

Serves: 4

Preferred spiralizer: Hourglass

Gluten-free

Good points: This recipe is very high in phosphorous

Nutritional Information Per Serving: Calories: 504;

Total Fat: 40.2g; Saturated Fat: 17.7g; Trans Fat: 0g;

Cholesterol: 83mg; Sodium: 851mg; Potassium: 337mg;

Total Carbs: 9.9g; Dietary Fiber: 0.6g; Sugar: 7.9g;

Protein: 26.3g; Vitamin A 19%; Calcium: 46%;

Vitamin C: 14%; Iron: 9%.

Ingredients

- 1 large zucchini, spiralized
- 6 strips of bacon
- 4 oz. of diced goat cheese
- 1 tablespoon of apple cider vinegar
- 3 tablespoons of extra virgin olive oil
- ½ teaspoon of whole grain Dijon mustard
- 2 tablespoons of maple syrup
- Salt and pepper, to taste

Directions:

1. Start by making the salsa. Combine 2 tablespoons of olive oil with the apple cider vinegar, the Dijon mustard, the maple syrup and sprinkle some salt and pepper to taste. Mix well and set aside.
2. Place a small pan over medium heat. Add a tablespoon of oil and fry the bacon strips. When crispy, take them out and place them on a paper towel lined plate.
3. In a large bowl, add the zucchini noodles and mix them with the bacon.
4. Pour over the sweet-sour dressing and toss to make sure they are well combined.
5. Transfer equal portions to the serving dishes. This goes great as a fresh side dish for other meals.

Simple Spiralized Jicama Snack

Prep Time: 5 minutes / Cook Time: 0 minutes

Serves: 4

Preferred spiralizer: Hourglass

Vegetarian-friendly

Good points: This recipe is very high in fiber and vitamin C, high in potassium, very low in saturated fat, and has no cholesterol

Nutritional Information Per Serving: Calories: 63;

Total Fat: 0.2g; Saturated Fat: 0g; Trans Fat: 0g;

Cholesterol: 0mg; Sodium: 45mg; Potassium: 249mg;

Total Carbs: 14.6g; Dietary Fiber: 8.1g; Sugar: 3g;

Protein: 1.2g; Vitamin A: 1%; Calcium: 2%;

Vitamin C: 56%; Iron: 6%

Ingredients:

- 1 jicama
- Sea salt, to taste
- Smoked paprika, to taste

Directions:

1. Peel the jicama using a vegetable peeler and then spiral into noodles.
2. Sprinkle with salt and the paprika.
3. Serve!

Zoodle Pesto Caprese Bites

Prep Time: 15 minutes / Cook Time: 15 minutes

Serves: 6

Preferred spiralizer: Hourglass

Vegetarian-friendly

Good points: This recipe is low in sugar, high in phosphorus, and very high in vitamin B6 and vitamin B12.

Nutritional Information Per Serving: Calories: 107;

Total Fat: 7.2g; Saturated Fat: 3.4g; Trans Fat: 0g;

Cholesterol: 16mg; Sodium: 204mg; Potassium: 68mg;

Total Carbs: 2.3g; Dietary Fiber: g; Sugar: 0.9g;

Protein: 8.8g; Vitamin A: 3%; Calcium: 4%;

Vitamin C: 7%; Iron: 1%

Ingredients:

- 1 beefsteak tomato, sliced into 3 pieces, 1/4-inch thick round slices, and then cut into halves
- 1/2 zucchini, medium-sized, spiralized using Blade A, noodles trimmed
- 2 tablespoons pesto sauce
- 6 pieces 1/4-inch thick round slices mozzarella, halved
- Olive oil, to drizzle, optional
- Salt and pepper, to garnish, optional

Directions:

1. In a medium-sized bowl, toss the zoodles with the pesto until well combined.
2. Put 1 piece of 1/2 a mozzarella slice into a clean surface. Add a tomato slice.
3. Roll up some zoodles and layer on top of the tomato slice. Top with another mozzarella slice.
4. Repeat the process until all the ingredients are used.
5. Transfer into a serving plate. If desired, drizzle with olive oil, pepper, and salt.

Oven Baked Ribbon Beet Chips

Prep Time: 20 minutes / Cook Time: 1 hour

Serves: 2

Preferred spiralizer: Hourglass

Vegan-friendly

Good points: This recipe is high in fiber, manganese, and potassium, and has no cholesterol

Nutritional Information Per Serving: Calories: 67;

Total Fat: 2.6g; Saturated Fat: 0g; Trans Fat: 0g;

Cholesterol: 0mg; Sodium: 659mg; Potassium: 318mg;

Total Carbs: 10.4; Dietary Fiber: 2.1g; Sugar: 8.1g;

Protein: 1.8g; Vitamin A: 1%; Calcium: 2%;

Vitamin C: 6%; Iron: 6%

Ingredients:

- 2 beets, medium-sized (about 1 pound)
- 1/4 teaspoon garlic powder
- 1/2 teaspoons kosher salt
- 1/2 teaspoon cumin powder
- 1 teaspoon extra-virgin olive oil

Directions:

1. Attach the ribbon blade of your vegetable spiralizer. Slice the beets into a thin long ribbon. Cut and separate the ribbon into individual round disks.
2. Put the beet slices into a large-sized mixing bowl. Add the salt, evenly toss, and let stand for at least 15 minutes. After 15 minutes, drain the liquid and transfer the beets into a salad spinner to remove any excess liquid.
3. Preheat the oven to 300F.
4. Transfer the beets into a clean large-sized mixing bowl. Add the rest of the ingredients. Gently massage the beets to coat them evenly with the seasoning and oil.
5. Spreading them in a single layer, put the beets into a parchment paper lined baking sheets, making sure that they are not overlapping. You may need 2 baking sheets for this.
6. Place the baking sheets in the bottom and middle rack of the oven. Bake for 1 hour and to ensure that they bake evenly, switch the 2 baking sheets between the bottom and middle rack every 20 minutes. If the chips seem soft after 1 hour, combine them into 1 baking sheet and bake on the middle rack for 10 minutes more - carefully watch to prevent the chips from burning.

7. Remove the baking sheet/s from the oven and let the chips rest on the baking sheet for 2 minutes and then transfer into a cooling rack.
8. If you have leftovers, store the chips in an airtight container for up to 7 days. If they become soft and slightly limp, bake them for 1 minute at 300F.

Chow Mein Zoodles

Prep Time: 1 hour, 20 minutes / Cook Time: 20 minutes

Serves: 6

Preferred spiralizer: Hourglass

Vegetarian-friendly

Good points: This recipe is very high in selenium, thiamin, vitamin B6, and vitamin C, and high in niacin, phosphorus, potassium, and riboflavin

Nutritional Information Per Serving: Calories: 87;

Total Fat: 4.2; Saturated Fat: 1.1g; Trans Fat: 0g;

Cholesterol: 19mg; Sodium: 749mg; Potassium: 323mg;

Total Carbs: 4.6g; Dietary Fiber: 1.4g; Sugar: 2.1g;

Protein: 8.2g; Vitamin A: 4%; Calcium: 3%;

Vitamin C: 29%; Iron: 4%

Ingredients:

- 3 yellow zucchinis, medium-sized
- 1 cup ground meat (beef, pork, turkey, chicken, or a mixture)
- 2 teaspoons toasted sesame oil
- 2 teaspoons sea salt
- 2 teaspoons lard or tallow
- 1/4 teaspoon white pepper powder
- 1/4 teaspoon sea salt
- 1/4 teaspoon fish sauce
- 1/2 tablespoon sesame seeds, toasted
- 1/2 onion, large-sized, chopped thinly against the grain
- 1 teaspoon ginger, freshly minced
- 1 stalk scallion, chopped thinly

- 1/2 teaspoon sriracha OR other chili sauce, optional
- Extra scallions and sesame seeds for garnishing, optional

Directions:

1. Mix the ground meat with the fish sauce, ginger, pepper, and salt. Cover and refrigerate for 1 hour.
2. Spiralize the zucchini into zoodles. Transfer the zoodles into a large-sized bowl, sprinkle with salt, and toss. Let stand for 20 to 30 minutes at room temperature to drain excess liquid.
3. After 20 to 30 minutes, drain the liquid and wash the salt off. Drain the zoodles well, spread them out into a large-sized clean towel. Keep the fridge for at least 1 hour to dehydrate further to make the zoodles firm.
4. In a frying pan, cook the marinated meat, breaking them apart using a spatula as it cooks, until stating to brown but not dry. Transfer to a bowl and set aside.
5. In the same pan, put 2 teaspoons of lard. Add the onion and fry gently until soft. Transfer into a small container and set aside.
6. In a large-sized and deep frying pan or a large-sized wok, put 2 teaspoons of lard and 2 teaspoons of sesame oil and heat over medium-high heat.
7. With a clean paper towel, blot the zoodles one last time. Toss the zoodles in the hot oil and stir fry for about 5 minutes or until soft. Toss in the cooked ground meat, cooked onions, scallions, and sesame seeds; toss for 30 seconds on high heat.
8. Transfer into a plate and immediately garnish with more sesame seeds and chopped scallions. Serve hot.
9. Serve with sriracha sauce or chopped thin fresh chilies, if desired.

Shrimp "Zoodle" Scampi

Prep Time: 10 minutes / Cook Time: 6 minutes

Serves: 4

Preferred spiralizer: Hourglass

Vegetarian-friendly

Good points: This recipe is very high in vitamin C and high in phosphorus, vitamin A, vitamin B6, and vitamin B12

Nutritional Information Per Serving: Calories: 303;

Total Fat: 14.1g; Saturated Fat: 8.1g; Trans Fat: 0g;

Cholesterol: 269mg; Sodium: 424mg; Potassium: 963mg;

Total Carbs: 13.4g; Dietary Fiber: 3.4g; Sugar: 6.1g;

Protein: 29.4g; Vitamin A: 38%; Calcium: 15%;

Vitamin C: 84%; Iron: 8%

Ingredients:

- 2 zucchinis
- 2 yellow squash
- 1 pound shrimp, peeled and then deveined
- 1 pint grape or cherry tomatoes, halved
- 1/4 cup white wine, plus more
- 1 lemon, juice only
- 4 garlic cloves, chopped
- 4 tablespoon butter
- Few shakes hot pepper flakes
- Handful fresh basil, sliced into chiffonade
- Kosher salt and pepper

Directions:

1. Spiralize the zucchini zoodles. Liberally season with the pepper and salt. Set aside.
2. In large-sized and heavy skillet, add the butter and heat on high heat. Add the shrimp and season with hot pepper flakes and cook for 3 minutes. Add the tomatoes and the zoodles. Add the fresh squeezed lemon and white wine in the pan. Cook for about 3 minutes or until the zoodles are soft.
3. With tongs, divide the zoodle mix between bowls and top with the basil chiffonade.

Spicy Carrot Noodles

Prep Time: 10 minutes / Cook Time: 20 minutes

Serves: 2

Preferred spiralizer: Hourglass

Gluten-free

Good points: This recipe is very high in vitamins A and C, as well being low in cholesterol

Nutritional Information Per Serving: Calories: 173;

Total Fat: 11.2g; Saturated Fat: 2.3g; Trans Fat: 0g;

Cholesterol: 11mg; Sodium: 372mg; Potassium: 510mg;

Total Carbs: 15.3g; Dietary Fiber: 3.2g; Sugar: 6.5g;

Protein: 4.9g; Vitamin A 373%; Calcium: 5%;

Vitamin C: 34%; Iron: 4%.

Ingredients

- 2 cups of carrots, spiralized
- 1 tablespoon of virgin olive oil
- 2 links of spicy sausage, de-cased
- 2 teaspoons. Of lime juice
- 1 red chili pepper
- 1/2 cup chicken broth
- 1/2 teaspoon chili powder
- Salt and pepper, to taste

Directions:

1. Place a medium-sized skillet over medium heat. Wait for the olive oil to heat up and then add the sausage meat. Cook until the meat becomes brown.
2. Add the chili pepper, finely sliced, and the chili powder. Mix well.
3. Add the spiralized carrots. After mixing them in, pour the chicken broth, and bring it to a boil.
4. Add salt and pepper to taste, and let it simmer for 10 minutes.
5. Before taking the skillet from the heat, pour the lime juice over the mixture.
6. Serve immediately.

Spiralized Sweet Potato Latkes

Prep Time: 10 minutes / Cook Time: 6 minutes per batch

Serves: 12

Preferred spiralizer: Hourglass

Vegetarian-friendly

Good points: This recipe is very high in vitamin B6 and high in selenium and vitamin C

Nutritional Information Per Serving: Calories: 106;

Total Fat: 6.9g; Saturated Fat: 1.4g; Trans Fat: 0g;

Cholesterol: 82mg; Sodium: 334mg; Potassium: 212mg;

Total Carbs: 8g; Dietary Fiber: 1.4g; Sugar: 2.3g;

Protein: 3.8g; Vitamin A: 7%; Calcium: 3%;

Vitamin C: 21%; Iron: 9%

Ingredients:

- 1 large-sized (about 11 ounces peeled) sweet potato, peeled
- 2 eggs, large-sized, beaten
- 1/2 cup scallions, chopped
- 1/2 teaspoon fresh black pepper, to taste
- 1/2 teaspoon kosher salt, to taste
- 4 cloves garlic, crushed
- 4 teaspoons olive oil

Directions:

1. Cut the potato into halves so it's easier to spiralize into noodles. Cut into about 5-inches long pieces.
2. In a large-sized bowl, mix the sweet potatoes with the eggs, scallions, garlic, pepper, and salt until well combined.
3. Over medium-low heat, heat a large-sized nonstick skillet. When hot, add 1 teaspoon oil and swirl around the pan. With a fork, grab about 1/3 cup of the sweet potato mix and gently place the skillet, pressing lightly down with the fork. You can fit 4 pieces' latkes in the skillet.
4. Cook for about 3 minutes or until the bottom is golden. Flip using a spatula and press down with the fork to flatten. Cook for about 3 minutes more or until golden.

Parmesan Pesto Zoodles with Tomato and Basil

Prep Time: 10 minutes / Cook Time: 15 minutes

Serves: 4

Preferred spiralizer: Hourglass

Vegetarian-friendly

Good points: This recipe is high in manganese, vitamin A, vitamin C, is low in sodium, and is very low in cholesterol

Nutritional Information Per Serving: Calories: 212;

Total Fat: 20.5g; Saturated Fat: 3.3g; Trans Fat: 0g;

Cholesterol: 4mg; Sodium: 97mg; Potassium: 390mg;

Total Carbs: 6.5g; Dietary Fiber: 1.8g; Sugar: 2.5g;

Protein: 4.2g; Vitamin A: 23%; Calcium: 9%;

Vitamin C: 39%; Iron: 6%

Ingredients:

- 2 zucchinis, medium-sized, spiraled into zoodles
- 1/2 teaspoon red pepper flakes, less or more to preference
- 1/2 cup shredded parmesan cheese
- 1/2 cup grape or cherry tomatoes, cut in half
- 1 tablespoon olive oil
- 1 tablespoon garlic, minced
- Salt and pepper, to taste

For the pesto:

- 1/4-1/3 cup olive oil
- 2 cups fresh basil leaves
- 2 teaspoons fresh, minced garlic
- 2-3 tablespoon pine nuts

Directions:

1. Put all the ingredients for the pesto in a blender and blend until processed to your desired consistency. Use 1/4 of the pesto and store the remaining in the fridge for up to 7 days.
2. In a large-sized pan, add the olive oil and heat. Add the garlic and tomatoes and sauté for a couple of minutes until heated.
3. Toss the zoodles in the pot and cook for about 5 minutes or until heated through.
4. Add the pesto, salt, pepper, red pepper flakes, and parmesan cheese. Continue cooking for a couple of minutes or until the cheese is melted.

5. Transfer to a serving plate. If desired, sprinkle the top with additional freshly grated parmesan cheese. Serve.

Zoodle, Feta and Thyme Triple-Cheese Bake

Prep Time: 15 minutes / Cook Time: 40-45 minutes

Serves: 4

Preferred spiralizer: Hourglass

Vegetarian-friendly

Good points: This recipe is very high vitamin B12 and high in calcium, phosphorus, vitamin B6, and vitamin C

Nutritional Information Per Serving: Calories: 415;

Total Fat: 31.5g; Saturated Fat: 12.8g; Trans Fat: 0g;

Cholesterol: 137mg; Sodium: 1324mg; Potassium: 670mg;

Total Carbs: 16.3g; Dietary Fiber: 4g; Sugar: 7.5g;

Protein: 21.8g; Vitamin A: 17%; Calcium: 46%;

Vitamin C: 64%; Iron: 18%

Ingredients:

- 2 zucchinis, medium-sized, trimmed and spiralized
- 1 egg
- 1 cup mozzarella cheese, grated
- 1/2 cup parmesan cheese, grated
- 1/2 cup feta cheese, crumbled
- 2 tablespoons olive oil or coconut oil
- 1/2 teaspoon salt
- 1/2 teaspoon black pepper
- 1 tablespoon thyme (fresh is preferred, but you can use dried)
- 1 onion, peeled and then chopped
- 1 clove garlic, peeled and then chopped

Directions:

1. Preheat the oven to 375F or 190C.
2. Put the spiralized zucchini in a colander and sprinkle with salt. Let stand for 10 minutes to draw and drain excess water out. After 10 minutes, gently wash the noodles and pat dry using a kitchen towel.
3. Put the olive oil in a frying pan and heat over medium heat. Add the garlic and onion. Sauté for about 3 to 4 minutes or until soft.
4. Add the zoodles. Cook for 4 minutes or until soft. Put the zucchini into an oven-safe bowl. Add the cheeses, crack the egg into the bowl, add the thyme, and season to taste. Mix until well combined
5. Bake for about 40-45 minutes.

Creamy Roasted Red Pepper Zucchini Noodles

Prep Time: 20 minutes / Cook Time: 10 minutes

Serves: 4

Preferred spiralizer: Hourglass

Vegetarian-friendly

Good points: This recipe is very high in vitamin C, high in vitamin B6, and low in cholesterol

Nutritional Information Per Serving: Calories: 269;

Total Fat: 21.8g; Saturated Fat: 5.9g; Trans Fat: 0g;

Cholesterol: 15mg; Sodium: 1014mg; Potassium: 811mg;

Total Carbs: 14.8g; Dietary Fiber: 3.7g; Sugar: 7.9g;

Protein: 8.4g; Vitamin A: 25%; Calcium: 17%;

Vitamin C: 203%; Iron: 9%

Ingredients:

For the creamy roasted red pepper sauce:

- 2 roasted red peppers, 8 ounces' total
- 2 ounces' goat cheese
- 1 teaspoon sea salt
- 1 tablespoon extra-virgin olive oil

For the Zucchini Noodles:

- 2 pounds' zucchini, ends trimmed off and then spiralized into noodles
- 2 cloves garlic, minced
- 1/4 cup extra-virgin olive oil
- 1/2 cup onion, minced
- 1 teaspoon sea salt

Serve with:

- Fresh parsley, chopped
- Parmesan, freshly grated
- Extra goat cheese
- Black pepper, freshly ground

Directions:

1. Put all the sauce ingredients into a blender and blend until the mixture is smooth.
2. Heat a large-sized, 15-inch, deep skillet on medium high heat. When the skillet is hot, add the olive oil, garlic, and onion. Sauté foe 1-2 minutes or until the onion is soft but not brown.
3. Add the salt and then the zoodles in the skillet. With a nonstick tong, toss the zoodles. Just as the zoodles are starting to become soft, but before they begin to shred water, add the sauce. Cook until just the sauce is heated.
4. Sprinkle with salt to taste. Serve immediately with parsley, goat cheese, parmesan, and black pepper.

SOUPS AND STEWS

Zucchini Noodles and Ginger Egg Soup

Prep Time: 10 minutes / Cook Time: 15 minutes

Serves: 2

Preferred spiralizer: Hourglass

Vegetarian-friendly

Good points: This recipe is very high in manganese, riboflavin and vitamin C

Nutritional Information Per Serving: Calories: 164;

Total Fat: 11.2g; Saturated Fat: 2.2g; Trans Fat: 0g;

Cholesterol: 93mg; Sodium: 1260mg; Potassium: 551mg;

Total Carbs: 6.9g; Dietary Fiber: 1.5g; Sugar: 2.8g;

Protein: 9.9g; Vitamin A 6%; Calcium: 4%;

Vitamin C: 28%; Iron: 10%.

Ingredients

- 1 large zucchini, spiralized
- 1 tablespoon of extra virgin olive oil
- 1 tablespoon of minced ginger
- 2 teaspoons of sherry vinegar
- 1 tablespoon soy sauce
- 2 cups vegetable broth
- 1 large egg, beaten
- Salt and pepper to taste

Directions:

1. Place a saucepan over medium heat. Cook the ginger in heated oil for two minutes. Add the sherry vinegar, the soy sauce and the broth and bring it to a boil.
2. While stirring continuously, add the beaten egg and make sure that it forms into small slices.
3. Add the zucchini noodles and cook for 5 minutes.
4. Remove from the heat and let it cool down before serving. Add salt and pepper, to taste.

Italian-Inspired Meatball Zoodle Soup

Prep Time: 30 minutes / Cook Time: 6 hours

Serves: 12

Preferred spiralizer: Hourglass

Vegetarian-friendly

Good points: This recipe is very high in vitamin B12, B6, iron, and selenium, and high in niacin, phosphorus, and zinc

Nutritional Information Per Serving: Calories: 145;

Total Fat: 5g; Saturated Fat: 2.1g; Trans Fat: 0g;

Cholesterol: 69mg; Sodium: 564mg; Potassium: 402mg;

Total Carbs: 3.8g; Dietary Fiber: 0.9g; Sugar: 1.5g;

Protein: 20.4g; Vitamin A: 23%; Calcium: 5%;

Vitamin C: 13%; Iron: 62%

Ingredients:

For the soup:

- 1 carrot, chopped
- 1 zucchini, medium-sized, spiraled
- 32 ounces' beef stock
- 1 onion, small sized, diced
- 1 tomato, medium-sized, diced
- 6 cloves garlic, minced
- 2 ribs celery, chopped
- 1 1/2 teaspoons sea salt

For the meatballs:

- 1 1/2-pound ground beef
- 1/2 cup Parmesan cheese, shredded
- 1 egg, large-sized
- 1 1/2 teaspoon garlic salt
- 1 1/2 teaspoon onion powder
- 1 teaspoon dried oregano
- 1 teaspoon Italian seasoning
- 1/2 teaspoon black pepper
- 4 tablespoons fresh parsley, chopped
- Olive oil, for frying the meatballs

Directions:

1. Heat a slow cooker on low setting.
2. Put all the soup ingredients in the slow cooker.
3. In a large-sized bowl, combine the meatball ingredients and mix until well combined. Form the mix into 30 meatballs.
4. Put the olive oil in a large-sized skillet and heat on medium-high heat. When the skillet is hot, add the meatballs in the skillet and brown all the sides – there is no need to cook them all the way through since you will add them in the slow cooker.
5. Add the meatballs into the slow cooker. Cover and cook for 6 hours on LOW.

Chicken Zoodle Soup

Prep Time: 5 minutes / Cook Time: 45 minutes

Serves: 5

Preferred spiralizer: Hourglass

Vegetarian-friendly

Good points: This recipe is high in niacin, selenium, vitamin A, vitamin C, and very high in magnesium and phosphorus

Nutritional Information Per Serving: Calories: 498;

Total Fat: 17.9g; Saturated Fat: 4.8g; Trans Fat: 0g;

Cholesterol: 180mg; Sodium: 1155mg; Potassium: 1405mg;

Total Carbs: 12.3g; Dietary Fiber: 3.2g; Sugar: 6g;

Protein: 68.6g; Vitamin A: 54%; Calcium: 40%;

Vitamin C: 65%; Iron: 12%

Ingredients:

- 4 zucchinis, medium-sized, ends trimmed and then cut vertically into halves
- 2 chicken breasts, cooked and then shredded (aim for 3 ounces per serving)
- 2 cloves garlic, minced
- 2 onions, medium-sized, sliced in very thin half-rounds
- 6 cups chicken stock or broth
- Handful baby carrots, sliced into 1/2-inch pieces
- Handful parsley, chopped
- Pepper

- Salt

Directions:

1. In a large-sized saucepan, add the chicken stock, carrots, garlic, and onion, and cook for 30 minutes or until the vegetables are fork tender.
2. Season the soup with pepper, salt, and parsley.
3. Spiralize the zucchini into noodles. Cut the long strands into shorter pieces.
4. Add the chicken and then the zucchini into the broth. Let stand until heated through.

Slow Cooked Miso Zoodle Vegetable Soup

Prep Time: 10 minutes / Cook Time: 3- 4 hours on HIGH; 6- 8 hours on LOW, plus 5-10 minutes

Serves: 4

Preferred spiralizer: Hourglass

Vegetarian-friendly

Good points: This recipe is very high in manganese, niacin, potassium, vitamin A, and vitamin C, and high in fiber, phosphorus, riboflavin, and vitamin B6, and has no cholesterol

Nutritional Information Per Serving: Calories: 76;

Total Fat: 1.8g; Saturated Fat: g; Trans Fat: 0g;

Cholesterol: 0mg; Sodium: 1126mg; Potassium: 561mg;

Total Carbs: 8.2g; Dietary Fiber: 2g; Sugar: 3.8g;

Protein: 6.9g; Vitamin A: 142%; Calcium: 8%;

Vitamin C: 46%; Iron: 7%

Ingredients:

- 1 zucchini, spiralized, for later
- 1/2 head Napa cabbage, shredded (about 2 cups)
- 2 carrots, peeled and sliced
- 1 tablespoon white miso paste
- 1/2 teaspoon ginger, minced
- 1/4 teaspoon salt

- 2 cloves garlic, minced
- 2 cups water
- 4 cups vegetable broth
- Large handful greens, for later (like spinach, kale, etc. I used a blend)

Directions:

1. Except for the zucchini and the greens, put the rest of the ingredients into a crockpot.
2. Stir to combine and then cook for 3 to 4 hours on HIGH or for 6 to 8 hours on LOW.
3. When the vegetables are cooked to desired tenderness, add the zucchini and greens. Let cook for another 5-10 minutes. Serve.

Kale Soup with Turnip Noodles and Scrambled Eggs

Prep Time: 10 minutes / Cook Time: 40 minutes

Serves: 5

Preferred spiralizer: Hand-crank

Vegetarian-friendly

Good points: This recipe is very high in niacin and vitamins A and C, as well as in manganese

Nutritional Information Per Serving: Calories: 166;

Total Fat: 8.6g; Saturated Fat: 1.7g; Trans Fat: 0g;

Cholesterol: 65mg; Sodium: 688mg; Potassium: 666mg;

Total Carbs: 14.7g; Dietary Fiber: 3.8g; Sugar: 5.6g;

Protein: 8.9g; Vitamin A 98%; Calcium: 10%;

Vitamin C: 98%; Iron: 12%

Ingredients

- 2 cups of kale, chopped
- 2 turnips, spiralized into noodles
- 2 tablespoons of olive oil
- 1 onion, chopped
- 3 garlic cloves, minced

- 4 cups of vegetable broth
- 2 cups of green beans
- 2 eggs
- 1 tablespoon of tomato paste
- 1 cup of tomatoes, chopped
- 1 tablespoon of chopped parsley
- Salt and pepper to taste

Directions:

1. Start by heating the oil in a medium-sized pot. Add the onion and sauté for a few minutes.
2. Add the garlic, the turnips and the kale, combine and cook for another 3 minutes.
3. Pour in the chopped tomatoes and the tomato paste. Stir everything well.
4. Add the vegetable broth, the beans and the parsley. Season it with salt, pepper, and cook for 25 minutes on low heat.
5. With 5 minutes to go, break the eggs into a bowl and beat them thoroughly. Add them to the soup and stir continuously for 2-3 minutes.
6. Remove from the heat and cover with a lid. Let it rest for a few minutes before serving.

Sausage, Carrot, and Spiralized Sweet Potato Soup

Prep Time: 10 minutes / Cook Time: 30 minutes

Serves: 5-8

Preferred spiralizer: Hourglass

Vegetarian-friendly

Good points: This recipe is very high in vitamin B6 and vitamin A.

Nutritional Information Per Serving: Calories: 345;

Total Fat: 23g; Saturated Fat: 8.3g; Trans Fat: 0g;

Cholesterol: 61mg; Sodium: 1224mg; Potassium: 581mg;

Total Carbs: 15g; Dietary Fiber: 4.2g; Sugar: 7.4g;

Protein: 19.4g; Vitamin A: 101%; Calcium: 14%;

Vitamin C: 30%; Iron: 20%

Ingredients:

- 1 pound fresh, raw, ground pork
- 1 cup half and half
- 1 sweet potato, medium-sized, spiralized
- 1 tablespoon olive oil
- 1 teaspoon thyme, dried
- 1/2 onion, medium-sized, chopped
- 1/2 teaspoon oregano, dried
- 3 carrot, medium-sized, chopped
- 3 clove garlic, minced
- 30 ounces canned crushed tomatoes
- 4 cup spinach
- 6 cup chicken broth, low-sodium

Serve with:

- 1/4 cup Parmesan cheese, grated
- 1 tablespoon parsley, fresh
- 1 lemon, medium-sized

Directions:

1. In a skillet, cook the sausage until browned and set aside on a plate lined with paper towels.
2. In a large-sized pot, put the olive oil and heat over medium-high heat. Add the onion and sauté until the onions are starting to become translucent. Add the garlic and carrot and sauté for about 2 to 3 minutes.
3. Add the cooked sausage, crushed tomatoes, and chicken broth and bring to a boil. Simmer for 5 minutes. Add the spiralized sweet potatoes and cook for 3 minutes more or until the sweet potatoes are soft to your preference.
4. Add the spinach and heat until just wilted. Add the half-and-half and bring to a boil until just heated through. Remove the pot from the heat. Serve garnished with the parsley, parmesan cheese, and lemon wedges.

Vegetable Soup with Corn Kernels and Carrot Noodles

Prep Time: 10 minutes / Cook Time: 35 minutes

Serves: 6

Preferred spiralizer: Hourglass

Vegetarian and Vegan friendly

Good points: This recipe is very high in niacin and vitamins A, B6 and C, as well as niacin and manganese. It has no cholesterol

Nutritional Information Per Serving: Calories: 131;

Total Fat: 5.9g; Saturated Fat: 1g; Trans Fat: 0g;

Cholesterol: 0mg; Sodium: 769mg; Potassium: 617mg;

Total Carbs: 15.3g; Dietary Fiber: 3.1g; Sugar: 5.1g;

Protein: 5.5g; Vitamin A 76%; Calcium: 4%;

Vitamin C: 24%; Iron: 9%

Ingredients

- 2 carrots, spiralized
- 1/2 cup of sweet corn kernels, drained
- 2 tablespoons of olive oil
- 1 onion, chopped
- 2 garlic cloves, minced
- 4 cups of vegetable broth
- 2 cups of celery, sliced
- 1 potato, diced
- 1 cup of tomato sauce
- Salt and pepper to taste
- 2 tablespoons of chopped parsley

Directions:

1. Start by heating the oil in a medium-sized pot. Add the onion and the celery and sauté for a few minutes.
2. Add the garlic, combine and cook for another minute.
3. Pour in the tomato sauce and the broth, stir well and let it simmer for 10 minutes.

4. Add the carrot noodles and the potatoes. Season everything with salt and pepper and turn the heat down. Cook for another 15 minutes.
5. Add the corn kernels and the parsley and cover the pot with a lid. Turn the heat off and let the soup rest for 5-10 minutes.
6. Remove the lid and transfer the soup to the serving bowls.

Spicy Chicken with Zucchini Noodles Soup

Prep Time: 20 minutes / Cook Time: 40 minutes

Serves: 4

Preferred spiralizer: Hourglass

Gluten free

Good points: This recipe is high in niacin, selenium and vitamins A, B6 and C

Nutritional Information Per Serving: Calories: 611;

Total Fat: 26.4g; Saturated Fat: 6.3g; Trans Fat: 0g;

Cholesterol: 202mg; Sodium: 1394mg; Potassium: 1557mg;

Total Carbs: 15.3g; Dietary Fiber: 4g; Sugar: 7.3g;

Protein: 76.1g; Vitamin A 115%; Calcium: 12%;

Vitamin C: 64%; Iron: 29%.

Ingredients

- 4 zucchinis, spiralized
- 2 pounds of chicken thighs, with the bone-in
- 1 stalk of celery, diced
- 2 medium-sized carrots, diced
- 3 garlic cloves, minced
- 1 small red onion, diced
- 6 cups of chicken broth
- 2 cups water
- ¼ teaspoon. of red pepper flakes
- 1 teaspoon of fresh thyme
- 1 tablespoon. of bay leaves
- 2 tablespoons of olive oil

- Salt and pepper to taste

Directions:

1. Heat the oil in a soup pot over medium heat. Add the onion, the garlic and the pepper flakes and stir for 2-3 minutes. Add the celery and the carrots and cook for another 5 minutes.
2. Put in the chicken thighs, the bay leaves and fresh thyme and mix well, before adding the broth and the water. Bring it to a boil and then let it simmer gently for another 30 minutes.
3. Add the spiralized zucchini and mix well. Take the pot off the heat and discard the bay leaves.
4. Serve hot.

Italian Beef, Carrots, and Spiralized Zucchini Soup

Prep Time: minutes / Cook Time: minutes

Serves: 8

Preferred spiralizer: Hourglass

Vegetarian-friendly

Good points: This recipe is very high in iron, vitamin A, vitamin B6, vitamin B12, and high in niacin, phosphorus, selenium, vitamin C, and zinc

Nutritional Information Per Serving: Calories: 342;

Total Fat: 16.1g; Saturated Fat: 5.8g; Trans Fat: 0g;

Cholesterol: 104mg; Sodium: 1171mg; Potassium: 1140mg;

Total Carbs: 11.4g; Dietary Fiber: 3.1g; Sugar: 6.6g;

Protein: 37.1g; Vitamin A: 90%; Calcium: 6%;

Vitamin C: 35%; Iron: 102%

Ingredients:

- 1 1/2 pounds ground beef, grass-fed
- 1/2 pound Italian pork sausage

- 1 bay leaf, large-sized
- 1 box (18 ounces) unsweetened tomato sauce
- 1 tablespoon butter, grass-fed OR ghee
- 1 teaspoon dried thyme
- 1/2 cup fresh basil, chopped, PLUS extra for topping, if desired
- 1/2 red onion, large-sized, chopped
- 2 1/2 tablespoons tomato paste
- 2 teaspoons dried oregano
- 3 carrots, large-sized, sliced
- 3 cloves garlic, large-sized, minced
- 3 stalks celery, chopped
- 3 zucchinis, medium-sized, spiralized into noodles
- 5 1/2 cups chicken and/or beef bone broth, preferably homemade
- Pinch cayenne pepper
- Raw parmesan cheese, for topping, optional
- Sea salt and black pepper to taste

Directions:

1. Put the butter in a large-sized soup pot and melt over medium heat. Add the carrots, celery, garlic, and onion. Sauté for a couple of minutes, occasionally stirring. Add the ground beef and pork sausage, breaking up the meat using a spatula. Add the cayenne, thyme, oregano, black pepper, and sea salt. Stir to combine.
2. When the meat is browned, add the tomato paste, tomato soup, broth and bay leaf. Stir well to combine. Add the zoodles and the fresh basil. Simmer for 25 minutes or until the zoodles are soft, tasting and adjusting the seasoning as needed.
3. When ready to serve, remove the bay leaf.
4. Garnish each serving with parmesan cheese and chopped basil, if desired.

Vegan Spiralized Zucchini, Tofu, Carrot and Kale Miso Soup

Prep Time: 20 minutes / Cook Time: 30 minutes

Serves: 6

Preferred spiralizer: Hourglass

Vegetarian and vegan-friendly

Good points: This recipe is very high in vitamin A and vitamin C, is high in calcium and manganese, and has no cholesterol

Nutritional Information Per Serving: Calories: 181;

Total Fat: 9.8g; Saturated Fat: 1.5g; Trans Fat: 0g;

Cholesterol: 0mg; Sodium: 524mg; Potassium: 600mg;

Total Carbs: 15.4g; Dietary Fiber: 4.6g; Sugar: 4.2g;

Protein: 11.1g; Vitamin A: 74%; Calcium: 19%;

Vitamin C: 41%; Iron: 16%

Ingredients:

- 1 cup bean sprouts
- 1 cup edamame, shelled
- 1 Japanese sweet potato, spiralized (OR 1 zucchini)
- 2 carrots, spiralized
- 7 ounces extra firm tofu, organic, drained and cubed
- 6 cups water
- 5 tablespoons white miso paste
- 4 large-sized stalks kale, stem removed and then thinly sliced
- 4 cloves garlic, minced
- 3 green onions, thinly sliced
- 2 tablespoons extra-virgin olive oil
- 2 stalks celery, thinly sliced
- 1 yellow onion, peeled and then diced
- 1 tablespoon fresh ginger, peeled and grated, PLUS more for serving
- Sea salt, to taste

Directions:

1. Put the oil into the large-sized pot and put over medium heat. Add the onion. Sauté for about 5 minutes or until soft. Add the garlic and ginger. Sauté for 1 minute. Add the carrots, sweet potato, and celery. Sauté for 2 minutes. Add the water and bring to a simmer. Cook until the vegetables are starting to become soft.
2. Carefully transfer 1 cup of warm water into a bowl and whisk in the miso paste. Pour the miso mix into the pot and stir to combine.
3. Gently simmer until the veggies are cooked through.
4. Add the tofu, edamame, and kale. Simmer for 1 minute or until the kale is wilted.
5. Remove from the heat and season with the salt to taste.
6. Top each serving with green onions and bean sprouts. If desired, grate a pinch of ginger over the top of each serving.

Spiralized Zucchini, Shiitake Mushrooms, and Bok Choy Ramen Soup

Prep Time: 15 minutes / Cook Time: 30 minutes

Serves: 3

Preferred spiralizer: Hourglass

Vegetarian-friendly

Good points: This recipe is very high in manganese, niacin, vitamin A, and vitamin C, and high in phosphorus, potassium, riboflavin, selenium, and vitamin B6 and has no cholesterol

Nutritional Information Per Serving: Calories: 147;

Total Fat: 5.7 g; Saturated Fat: 1.1g; Trans Fat: 0g;

Cholesterol: 0mg; Sodium: 1858mg; Potassium: 766mg;

Total Carbs: 15.1g; Dietary Fiber: 3.3g; Sugar: 5.5g;

Protein: 10.4g; Vitamin A: 64%; Calcium: 12%;

Vitamin C: 74%; Iron: 13%

Ingredients:

- 1 large-sized zucchini OR 2 small-sized zucchinis, trimmed and noodled using the Blade D
- 3 1/2 ounces' shiitake mushrooms, halved
- 7 ounces' baby bok choy, leaves separated and ends trimmed
- 4 cups vegetable stock
- 2 teaspoons sesame oil
- 2 tablespoons soy sauce, low-sodium
- 2 scallions, diced, green and white parts separated
- 1/4 teaspoon black sesame seeds PLUS 1/4 teaspoon white sesame seeds, mixed together
- 1/2 yellow onion, cut into 1/2" slices
- 1/2 tablespoon yellow or white miso paste
- 1 inch piece of ginger, peeled and minced
- 1 garlic clove, minced
- Hot sauce, to garnish, optional

Directions:

1. Put 1/2 of the oil in a large-sized skillet and heat over medium-high heat.
2. While the oil is heating up, rub the bok choy with the mixed paste using your fingers to completely cover.
3. When the oil is heated, add the bok choy and cook each side for 3 minutes or until browned. Remove the bok choy and set aside. Immediately add the remaining 1/2 of the oil, garlic, onion, ginger, and white scallions. Cook for about 5 minutes or until the onions are soft.
4. Pour the tock and soy sauce in the skillet. Cover and bring the boil. Add the mushrooms, lower the heat to a simmer and cook for 5 minutes or until the mushrooms are soft.
5. Add the zucchini noodles. Cook for 2 to 3 minutes or until the zoodles are cooked al dente to your preference.
6. With pasta tongs, transfer the zoodles carefully between 3 serving bowls. Top with the bok choy. Ladle the broth mixture over the bowls. Garnish with sesame seeds, green scallions, and, if desired, with hot sauce.
7. Serve immediately.

Beef Stew with Zucchini Noodles

Prep Time: 20 minutes / Cook Time: 80 minutes

Serves: 5

Preferred spiralizer: Hourglass

Paleo-friendly

Good points: This recipe is very high in iron, zinc and vitamins A, B6 and B12

Nutritional Information Per Serving: Calories 528;

Total Fat: 24.1g; Saturated Fat: 6.3g; Trans Fat: 0g;

Cholesterol: 162mg; Sodium: 839mg; Potassium: 1562mg;

Total Carbs: 14.7g; Dietary Fiber: 3.8g; Sugar: 8.2g;

Protein: 61.8g; Vitamin A 111%; Calcium: 7%;

Vitamin C: 71%; Iron: 200%

Ingredients:

- 2 pounds of beef, cut into chunks
- 3 medium-sized Zucchinis, spiralized
- 1 medium onion, diced
- 2 garlic cloves, minced
- 2 celery stalks, sliced
- 2 carrots, diced
- 2 tablespoons of Worcestershire sauce
- 14 oz. of tomatoes, peeled and diced, from the can
- 4 cups of beef broth
- 2 teaspoons of bay leaves
- 1/2 cup of parsley, chopped
- 1 teaspoon of chili flakes
- 1 teaspoon of thyme
- 4 tablespoons of olive oil
- Salt and pepper to taste

Directions:

1. Heat the olive oil in a large saucepan. Add the chunks of beef and cook until they are easily browned.
2. Add the garlic, the onion, and the chili flakes and cook for another two minutes.
3. Put in the celery stalks and the carrots and cook for five more minutes.
4. Mix the Worcestershire sauce, the bay leaves and the thyme and season with salt and pepper.
5. Pour in the beef broth and the can of diced tomatoes and bring to a boil. Afterwards, let it simmer for another 60-70 minutes, and let the stew thicken.
6. Put the zucchini spirals on the serving dishes and pour over the stew. Sprinkle the parsley over.

MEAT AND POULTRY

Sun-Dried Tomato and Basil Pesto Zoodles

Prep Time: 15 minutes / Cook Time: 8-10 minutes

Serves: 3-4

Preferred spiralizer: Hourglass

Vegetarian and paleo-friendly

Good points: This recipe is high in vitamin C, niacin, and manganese

Nutritional Information Per Serving: Calories: 523;

Total Fat: 37.9g; Saturated Fat: 5.4g; Trans Fat: 0g;

Cholesterol: 87mg; Sodium: 1031mg; Potassium: 1062mg;

Total Carbs: 12.2g; Dietary Fiber: 3.8g; Sugar: 5.8g;

Protein: 38.1g; Vitamin A: 22%; Calcium: 7%;

Vitamin C: 84%; Iron: 16%

Ingredients:

- 3-4 zucchini, large-sized
- 3/4 pound baked chicken, optional
- 1/4 teaspoon sea salt, PLUS more to taste
- 1/2 cup sun-dried tomatoes
- 1 cup 5-minute dairy free pesto, less or more to taste, recipe below

For the 5-minute dairy free pesto:

- 3/4 cup fresh basil
- 2 teaspoons minced garlic
- 1/4 cup pine nuts
- 1/4 cup + 2 tablespoons extra-virgin olive oil
- 1/2 teaspoon lemon juice
- 1 teaspoon salt

Directions:

For the 5-minute dairy free pesto:

1. Put 2 tablespoons of olive oil in a small-sized pan. Add the pine nuts. Toast for 5 minutes or until fragrant and slightly brown.
2. Put the pine nuts into a food processor and add the rest of the ingredients. Pulse until creamy and smooth, scraping down the edges using a spatula as needed.
3. Store in airtight container and keep in the fridge until ready to use.

For the zoodles:

1. If using chicken, bake the meat per your liking.
2. Spiralize the zucchini into noodles. Remove or peel the skin, as desired.
3. Put 1 to 2 tablespoons into a large-sized pan and melt over low-medium heat.
4. Toss the zucchini in the pan and cover. Cook for about 8-10 minutes, occasionally stirring, until cooked to your desired doneness.
5. Remove from the heat, but leave the zoodles in the pan. Season with the salt.
6. Mix in as much of the pesto to your liking. Mix in the sundried tomatoes and, if using, add the chicken now or later to top during serving time.

Fried Chicken with Potato Noodles and Basil

Prep Time: 20 minutes / Cook Time: 35 minutes

Serves: 6

Preferred spiralizer: Hourglass

Paleo-friendly

Good points: This recipe is very high in vitamins B6, B12 and C, and low in saturated fat

Nutritional Information Per Serving: Calories: 166;

Total Fat: 7.2g; Saturated Fat: 1.3g; Trans Fat: 0g;

Cholesterol: 25mg; Sodium: 96mg; Potassium: 527mg;

Total Carbs: 15.2g; Dietary Fiber: 2.7g; Sugar: 3.1g;

Protein: 10.6g; Vitamin A 22%; Calcium: 7%;

Vitamin C: 97%; Iron: 6%

Ingredients

- 2 lbs. of chicken breast, cut into strips
- 2 medium-sized potatoes, spiralized
- 1 medium red bell pepper, sliced
- ½ onion, sliced
- 2 garlic cloves, minced
- 1 cup of cherry tomatoes, halved
- ½ cup of chicken broth
- 2 tablespoons of extra virgin olive oil
- ½ teaspoon of paprika
- 1/2 cup of basil, chopped
- Salt and pepper, to taste

Directions:

1. Place a skillet over medium heat. Wait until the olive oil heats up and then add the chicken breast strips.
2. Season them with salt, pepper and paprika, and cook for 5 minutes.
3. Add in the red bell pepper and the onion, and cook for another five minutes.
4. Add the garlic, the tomatoes and the chicken broth. Lower the heat and let it simmer for another 15 minutes.
5. Add the potato noodles and mix well. Let it cook over low heat for ten minutes.
6. Set aside, sprinkle the chopped basil on top, and serve.

Sweet Potato Noodles with Minced Meat

Prep Time: 20 minutes / Cook Time: 20 minutes

Serves: 4

Preferred spiralizer: Hand-crank

Paleo-friendly, Gluten-free

Good points: This recipe is very high in vitamins B6, B12 and C, as well as in iron and selenium

Nutritional Information Per Serving: Calories: 529;

Total Fat: 21.4g; Saturated Fat: 6.4g; Trans Fat: 0g;

Cholesterol: 203mg; Sodium: 261mg; Potassium: 1167mg;

Total Carbs: 9.8g; Dietary Fiber: 1.6g; Sugar: 3g;

Protein: 70.5g; Vitamin A 8%; Calcium: 1%;

Vitamin C: 26%; Iron: 247%.

Ingredients

- 2 lbs. of beef mince
- 1 large sweet potato, peeled and spiralized into large noodles
- 1 garlic clove, minced
- 1/4 teaspoon red pepper flakes
- 1/2 cup beef broth
- ½ cup of freshly chopped basil
- 2 tablespoons of olive oil
- Salt and pepper, to taste

Directions:

1. Place a large pan over medium heat. Pour the garlic into the heated oil and add the pepper flakes. Fry them for no more than a minute.
2. Add the minced meat and cook until brown.
3. Mix in the sweet potato noodles and cook until crispy.
4. Pour in the broth and reduce it for 10 minutes.
5. Add salt and pepper to taste
6. Upon removing the pan from the heat, add in the chopped basil.
7. Serve right away.

Zucchini Noodles with Turkey Shreds

Prep Time: 15 minutes / Cook Time: 40 minutes

Serves: 4

Preferred spiralizer: Hourglass

Paleo-friendly

Good points: This recipe is very high in vitamins A, B6, B12 and C, and low in sodium

Nutritional Information Per Serving: Calories: 502;

Total Fat: 17.5g; Saturated Fat: 4.9g; Trans Fat: 0g;

Cholesterol: 168mg; Sodium: 234mg; Potassium: 1544mg;

Total Carbs: 15.7g; Dietary Fiber: 4.5g; Sugar: 8.3g;

Protein: 69.3g; Vitamin A 77%; Calcium: 11%;

Vitamin C: 84%; Iron: 25%.

Ingredients:

- 4 medium-sized zucchinis, spiralized
- 2 lbs. ground turkey breast, shredded
- 1 red onion, diced
- 1 carrot, diced
- 1 celery stalk, diced
- ½ teaspoon of red hot pepper flakes
- 2 cloves of garlic, minced
- 1 can of crushed tomatoes
- 1 tablespoon. tomato paste
- 1/4 cup chicken broth
- 1/4 cup chopped basil
- Salt and pepper to taste

Directions:

1. Place a large skillet over medium heat. Heat the olive oil and put in the red pepper flakes, together with the onion and the garlic. Cook for 3 minutes
2. Add the carrots and the celery. Cook for another 5 minutes.
3. Put in the shredded turkey and mix well. Season the mixture with salt and pepper.
4. Pour in the chicken broth and let it reduce for a few minutes.
5. Add the crushed tomatoes and the tomato paste. Bring to a boil and let it simmer for ten minutes.
6. Add the zucchini and mix with care. Let it boil for another five minutes.
7. Right before the end, add the chopped basil and set aside. Serve right away!

Spiralized Zucchini and Turkey Spaghetti

Prep Time: 10 minutes / Cook Time: 15-20 minutes

Serves: 4

Preferred spiralizer: Hourglass

Vegetarian-friendly

Good points: This recipe is very high in vitamin and high in niacin, potassium, selenium, and vitamin B6

Nutritional Information Per Serving: Calories: 217;

Total Fat: 10.5g; Saturated Fat: 1.9g; Trans Fat: 0g;

Cholesterol: 62mg; Sodium: 338mg; Potassium: 866mg;

Total Carbs: 15.6g; Dietary Fiber: 3.8g; Sugar: 9.2g;

Protein: 19g; Vitamin A: 14%; Calcium: 6%;

Vitamin C: 58%; Iron: 13%

Ingredients:

- 4 zucchinis, large-sized
- 8 ounces ground turkey
- 1 cup marinara sauce
- 1 tablespoon Italian seasoning
- 1 teaspoon extra-virgin olive oil
- Preferred spices, for the beef (I used An Evening in Tuscany by the Milford Spice Company)
- Parmesan or feta cheese, for sprinkle

Directions:

1. Break up any clump ground turkey meat and season with your desired spices. Cook in a skillet on medium high heat until the meat is no longer pink.
2. Wash the zucchini, cut the ends off, and spiralize into noodles. With a scissor, cut the zoodles into shorter strands.
3. Put the olive oil in a skillet and add the zoodles, sauté for about 3 to 5 minutes over high heat or until softened. Stir in the turkey and the sauce. Sprinkle with cheese and serve.

Cilantro Lime Chicken Zucchini

Prep Time: 10 minutes / Cook Time: 25-30 minutes

Serves: 4

Preferred spiralizer: Hourglass

Vegetarian-friendly

Good points: This recipe is very high in niacin, high in selenium, vitamin B6, and vitamin C, and is low in sugar and sodium.

Nutritional Information Per Serving: Calories: 381;

Total Fat: 15.1g; Saturated Fat: 3.5g; Trans Fat: 0g;

Cholesterol: 131mg; Sodium: 117mg; Potassium: 746mg;

Total Carbs: 9.9g; Dietary Fiber: 4.2g; Sugar: 1.6g;

Protein: 51.3g; Vitamin A: 6%; Calcium: 5%;

Vitamin C: 39%; Iron: 12%

Ingredients:

- 2 pieces' whole chicken breasts, sliced into 4 pieces
- 2-4 zucchini
- 1/4 cup cilantro, snipped
- 3-4 lime, juice
- 4-6 garlic cloves, minced
- Avocado, optional
- Cumin
- Olive oil

Directions:

1. Prepare the lime, garlic, and cilantro.
2. Coat the chicken with fresh squeezed lime juice. If desired, slice a lime into wedges and cut the avocado and out on the table.
3. Also, if you want, slice the chicken into chunks. You can skip this and cook them whole, but chunks cook faster.
4. Pour a small amount of olive oil in a sauté pan or a large-sized skillet, just enough to cover the bottom of the pan. Heat the oil over medium high heat.

5. When hot, put the chicken in the skillet, arranging them in a single layer. When the bottom of the chicken pieces are browned, sprinkle the top with cumin to taste and continue cooking until the chicken is half-cooked or half of the chicken is white and no longer pink.
6. While the chicken is cooking, spiralizer the zucchini into zoodles and cut them into shorter strands using a scissor.
7. Flip the chicken and cook for a couple of minutes more or until both sides are browned.
8. Reduce the heat and sprinkle the garlic and lemon zest in the pan. Stir and sauté for a bit or until the garlic is fragrant and a bit browned, but not burnt.
9. When the chicken is cooked, add the lime juice and stir to combine.
10. Transfer the chicken mix into a bowl.
11. Carefully put a little olive oil in the pan. Add in the zucchini. Cook, tossing, until the zoodles are a bit brown. Season to taste as desired.
12. Return the chicken in the pan and mix to combine. Add the cilantro. Serve.

Spicy Pork Chops with Zucchini Noodles

Prep Time: 10 minutes / Cook Time: 20 minutes

Serves: 2

Preferred spiralizer: Hand-crank

Gluten-free

Good points: This recipe is very high in selenium and low in sodium and sugar

Nutritional Information Per Serving: Calories: 425;

Total Fat: 37.1g; Saturated Fat: 11.3g; Trans Fat: 0g;

Cholesterol: 76mg; Sodium: 88mg; Potassium: 561mg;

Total Carbs: 4.8g; Dietary Fiber: 1.4g; Sugar: 1.8g;

Protein: 19.5g; Vitamin A 6%; Calcium: 6%;

Vitamin C: 33%; Iron: 10%.

Ingredients:

- 2 large pork chops, boneless
- 1 zucchini, spiralized
- 1 teaspoon of chili flakes

- ½ teaspoon of cumin
- ½ teaspoon of sage
- ½ teaspoon of thyme
- 2 garlic cloves
- 1/2 tablespoon of butter
- 2 tablespoons of olive oil
- Salt and pepper to taste

Directions:

1. Season the pork chops with salt and pepper. Add the chili flakes, the cumin, the sage and the thyme. Make sure the meat has a generous coating.
2. Heat some olive oil in a large pan over medium heat. Add the pork chops and cook for 3 minutes on each side.
3. Add the butter and the garlic. Once the butter melts, use a spoon to continuously coat the meat. Cook for another 4 minutes on each side.
4. Take the pork chops from the pan and into the serving plates. Drizzle over the melted butter. Discard the garlic cloves and let the meat rest for a few minutes before serving.
5. While the chops are resting, heat the rest of the olive oil over medium heat and cook the zucchinis. Sprinkle some salt and pepper and cook for 3-5 minutes.
6. Remove from the heat and place the zucchini next to the meat. Serve right away!

Pork Chops with Cucumber Noodles and Avocado Salad

Prep Time: 10 minutes / Cook Time: 15 minutes

Serves: 2

Preferred spiralizer: Hourglass

Gluten-free

Good points: This recipe is very low in sodium and sugar

Nutritional Information Per Serving: Calories: 593;

Total Fat: 53.6g; Saturated Fat: 13.6g; Trans Fat: 0g;

Cholesterol: 69mg; Sodium: 65mg; Potassium: 881mg;

Total Carbs: 11g; Dietary Fiber: 7.2g; Sugar: 1.5g;

Protein: 20.6g; Vitamin A 13%; Calcium: 6%;

Vitamin C: 23%; Iron: 10%.

Ingredients:

- 2 medium-sized pork chops
- 1 large avocado, diced
- 1 cup of cucumber, spiralized into large noodles
- ½ cup of Rocket, chopped
- ½ cup of Basil, chopped
- 2 tablespoons of olive oil
- 1 tablespoon of balsamic vinegar
- Salt and pepper

Directions:

1. Season the pork chops with salt and pepper.
2. Heat a grill pan, and when hot, add the pork chops. Cook them for five minutes on each side. If they are not thick, you can reduce the cooking time to just four minutes on each side.
3. Take the pork chops of the heat and set them aside.
4. In a large salad bowl, mix the avocado, the cucumber noodles, the basil and the rocket. Add the oil and the balsamic vinegar. Toss well and season with salt.
5. Transfer the salad to the serving plates, near the pork chops.

Zucchini with Chicken and Pistachios

Prep Time: 15 minutes / Cook Time: 15-20 minutes

Serves: 3-4

Preferred spiralizer: Hourglass

Vegetarian-friendly

Good points: This recipe is high in niacin, selenium, vitamin B6, and vitamin C, and low in sugar

Nutritional Information Per Serving: Calories: 502;

Total Fat: 19.6g; Saturated Fat: 3.7g; Trans Fat: 0g;

Cholesterol: 175mg; Sodium: 3295mg; Potassium: 1017 mg;

Total Carbs: 11.9g; Dietary Fiber: 3.9g; Sugar: 3.4g;

Protein: 69.9g; Vitamin A: 10%; Calcium: 12%;

Vitamin C: 52%; Iron: 33%

Ingredients:

For the noodles:

- 2-2 1/2 pounds (about 1 kilogram) zucchini
- 2 cloves garlic
- 1/4 teaspoon ground cumin
- 1/4 teaspoon ground black pepper
- 1 tablespoon salt
- 1 tablespoon extra-virgin olive oil

For the chicken:

- 4 chicken breasts, boneless, skinless (150 grams or 4-6 ounces each)
- 1/2 teaspoon ground black pepper
- 1 teaspoon salt
- 1 tablespoon extra-virgin olive oil OR ghee

Aromatics:

- 2 scallions
- 7-10 fresh mint leaves
- 1/4 cup pistachios, shelled
- 1 tablespoon lemon juice

Directions:

For the noodles:

1. With a spiralizer, julienne the zucchini. Put the zoodles into a colander and sprinkle with salt. Toss to combine until the zoodles are lightly coated. Set the colander in a sink and let drain.

For the chicken:

1. Put the chicken a chicken piece between two pieces' plastic wrap and pound the chicken pieces into 1/2-inch thickness using the smooth side of a meat hammer, then slice crosswise into strips. Repeat the process with the remaining chicken

pieces. Put the olive oil in a large-sized, nonstick skillet and heat over medium high heat, about 2 to 3 minutes. Put the chicken in the skillet, sprinkle with pepper and salt, and toss to coat with the oil.

2. Spread the chicken in a single layer in the skillet and cook for 2 to 3 minutes, undisturbed. Using a spatula, flip, separating the pieces, and cook for another 2 to 3 minutes. Continue and cook the chicken until most sides are browned and sizzling, for about 2 more minutes. Transfer the cooked chicken into a plate and loosely cover with aluminum foil.

For the aromatics:

1. Mince the mint leaves, thinly slice the scallions, and coarsely chop the pistachios. Put all the aromatics in a bowl and mix with the fork. Set the bowl nearby

To complete the dish:

1. Put the olive oil in a small-sized olive oil. Peel the garlic cloves and then crush them. Add the garlic into the bowl with the olive oil. Add the pepper and cumin into the bowl and mix using a fork; set aside nearby.
2. Rinse the zoodles under running water. Drain them well and squeeze them between clean a dish towel to remove excess water. Return the skillet where the chicken was cooked on the stovetop and reheat for about 2 to 3 minutes over medium-high heat.
3. Put the zoodles in the pan and sauté for about 2 to 3 minutes or until tender. Push side to one side of the skillet. Put the garlic oil in the cleared space in the skillet and cook for 20 seconds, constantly stirring.
4. Push the zoodles into the garlic oil and gently stir to coat with the oil.
5. Turn off the heat. Add the chicken and the pistachio mix. Toss to combine.

Pork Tenderloin with Green Olives and Roasted Potato Noodles

Prep Time: 10 minutes / Cook Time: 45 minutes

Serves: 8

Preferred spiralizer: Hand-crank

Gluten-free

Good points: This recipe is very high in thiamin, vitamins B6 and C, and low in sugar

Nutritional Information Per Serving: Calories: 268;

Total Fat: 8.4g; Saturated Fat: 2g; Trans Fat: 0g;

Cholesterol: 83mg; Sodium: 167mg; Potassium: 869mg;

Total Carbs: 14.6g; Dietary Fiber: 2.5g; Sugar: 1.6g;

Protein: 31.4g; Vitamin A 5%; Calcium: 3%;

Vitamin C: 32%; Iron: 12%

Ingredients:

- 2 pounds of pork tenderloin
- 1 cup of cherry tomatoes, halved
- 3 oz. of green olives, without kernel and halved
- 2 garlic cloves, minced
- 1 teaspoon of rosemary
- 3 potatoes, spiralized
- ¼ cup of dry white wine
- 2 tablespoons of olive oil
- Salt and pepper to taste

Directions:

1. Preheat the oven to 400 degrees Fahrenheit.
2. In a large bowl, mix the tomatoes, the olives, the garlic, the rosemary and the white wine.
3. Heat the olive oil in a large pan. Season the tenderloin with salt and pepper and place it into the pan. Cook for three minutes on each side.
4. Add the mixture from the bowl and the potato noodles to the pan and place it into the oven. Bake for 30-40 minutes.
5. Remove the pan from the oven and let it rest for a few minutes before serving.

Zucchini Noodles with Chicken and Mozzarella

Prep Time: 10 minutes / Cook Time: 15 minutes

Serves: 2

Preferred spiralizer: Hourglass

Gluten-free

Good points: This recipe is very high in calcium and vitamin C, and very low in sugar

Nutritional Information Per Serving: Calories: 330;

Total Fat: 12g; Saturated Fat: 4.7g; Trans Fat: 0g;

Cholesterol: 120mg; Sodium: 412mg; Potassium: 643mg;

Total Carbs: 5.7g; Dietary Fiber: 1.5g; Sugar: 1.9g;

Protein: 50.3g; Vitamin A 40%; Calcium: 35%;

Vitamin C: 41%; Iron: 12%.

Ingredients:

- 1 large zucchini, spiralized
- ½ lb. of chicken breast, cut into strips
- 1 cup of baby spinach
- 3 oz. of mozzarella cheese
- ¼ teaspoon. of red pepper flakes
- 1 tablespoon of lemon juice
- Salt and pepper, to taste

Directions:

1. Cook the chicken in a large saucepan over medium heat for five minutes.
2. When it is almost done, add the spiralized zucchini, the spinach and the lemon juice.
3. Season with salt, pepper and the red pepper flakes, and cook for another 3 to 5 minutes.
4. Remove from the heat and place the mixture onto the serving plates.
5. Top it with mozzarella cubes and serve immediately.

Pork Chops with Zucchini Spirals, Parmesan and Pistachio Salsa

Prep Time: 20 minutes / Cook Time: 25 minutes

Serves: 4

Preferred spiralizer: Hourglass

Gluten-free

Good points: This recipe is very high in phosphorous and vitamin C, and low in sugar

Nutritional Information Per Serving: Calories: 646;

Total Fat: 55.1g; Saturated Fat: 15.6g; Trans Fat: 0g;

Cholesterol: 89mg; Sodium: 386mg; Potassium: 1015mg;

Total Carbs: 11.9g; Dietary Fiber: 3.6g; Sugar: 4.7g;

Protein: 31.7g; Vitamin A 20%; Calcium: 33%;

Vitamin C: 79%; Iron: 12%.

Ingredients:

- 4 pork chops, boneless
- 3 large zucchinis, spiralized
- ½ cup of olive oil
- ½ cup of pistachios, pre-roasted
- 2 garlic cloves, minced
- 4 oz. Parmesan cheese, grated
- 1/4 cup of parsley, chopped
- Salt and pepper to taste

Directions:

1. Preheat the oven to 375F.
2. Season the pork chops with salt and pepper. Heat some olive oil in a skillet and sear the chops over medium heat, for 3 minutes on each side.
3. Take the skillet and place it in the oven. Bake the pork chops for 10 minutes. Next, take them out and place them aside.
4. While the pork chops are resting, prepare the salsa for the zucchini spirals.
5. Place the pistachio in a food processor, together with the remaining olive oil, the garlic cloves, the Parmesan cheese and the parsley.
6. In a large mixing bowl, place the zucchini spirals. Pour over the salsa and mix well.
7. Place the mixture on the serving dish next to the pork chops. Serve immediately.

FISH AND SEAFOOD

Creamy Yellow Squash Noodles, Mushrooms and Shrimp

Prep Time: 15 minutes / Cook Time: 15 minutes

Serves: 5

Preferred spiralizer: Hourglass

Vegetarian-friendly

Good points: This recipe is very high in vitamin B6, and high in niacin, phosphorus, vitamin A, vitamin B12, and vitamin C

Nutritional Information Per Serving: Calories: 304;

Total Fat: 11.7g; Saturated Fat: 6.2g; Trans Fat: 0g;

Cholesterol: 287mg; Sodium: 441mg; Potassium: 1026mg;

Total Carbs: 14.4g; Dietary Fiber: 4.3g; Sugar: 5.6g;

Protein: 37.1g; Vitamin A: 37%; Calcium: 18%;

Vitamin C: 57%; Iron: 18%

Ingredients:

- 1 1/2 pounds' raw shrimp, peeled and then deveined
- 4 yellow squash, small-sized, spiralized into noodles
- 2 tablespoons PLUS 1 teaspoon coconut oil, avocado oil, OR olive oil
- 2 garlic cloves, minced
- 2 cups fresh baby spinach
- 1/4 cup coconut OR almond flour
- 1/2-pound button mushrooms, chopped
- 1/2 cup coconut cream
- 1/2 cup chicken OR vegetable broth, low sodium
- 1 yellow onion, small-sized, sliced

Directions:

1. Put 2 tablespoons of oil in a large-sized skillet and heat over medium-high heat. Season the shrimp with salt and pepper. When the skillet is hot, put the shrimp and cook each side for 2 minutes or until translucent.
2. Transfer the shrimp into a plate and set aside.
3. In the same skillet, put 1 teaspoon oil and heat. Add the mushrooms, garlic, and onion. Sauté for about 4 minutes or until golden. Transfer into a plate and set aside.
4. Reduce the heat to medium low. Add the broth and then the cream. Bring the sauce to a boil and increase the heat to medium-low. Add the flour and briskly whisk until incorporated. Add the squash noodles and spinach and let the sauce bubble for about 3 minutes.
5. Return the shrimp and the mushrooms into the skillet.
6. Gently combine, combine, and turn of the heat. Turn the heat off and let rest for about 4 to 5 minutes.
7. Sprinkle with parmesan cheese and/or freshly-chopped parsley.

Zucchini Spirals with Mussels and Chorizo

Prep Time: 10 minutes / Cook Time: 20 minutes

Serves: 4

Preferred spiralizer: Hourglass

Gluten-free, Paleo-friendly

Good points: This recipe is rich in vitamins B6, B12 and C, as well as in iron and phosphorus

Nutritional Information Per Serving: Calories: 283;

Total Fat: 15.8g; Saturated Fat: 3.7g; Trans Fat: 0g;

Cholesterol: 47mg; Sodium: 547mg; Potassium: 991mg;

Total Carbs: 14.5g; Dietary Fiber: 2.8g; Sugar: 4.9g;

Protein: 20.6g; Vitamin A 20%; Calcium: 7%;

Vitamin C: 73%; Iron: 32%

Ingredients:

- 3 large zucchinis, spiralized

- 30-40 mussels, cleaned
- 1 link of chorizo, sliced
- 1 small red onion, diced
- 2 cloves of garlic, minced
- 1 cup of cherry tomatoes, halved
- 2 tablespoons of olive oil
- 1/2 cup of basil, chopped
- Salt and pepper, to taste

Directions:

1. In a medium-sized skillet, heat the olive oil and add the chorizo. Cook it for a few minutes, until brown.
2. Add the onion, the garlic and cook for another 3 minutes.
3. Pour in the cherry tomatoes, add salt and pepper and cover the skillet. Cook for 5 minutes.
4. Add the mussels and the basil and let it cook for 2-3 minutes, or until the mussels open. Remember to remove the ones that remain closed.
5. Place the zucchini noodles on the serving dishes and pour over the sauce.
6. Let it sit for a few minutes, before serving. Enjoy!

Parsnip Pasta with Salmon and Leeks

Prep Time: 10 minutes / Cook Time: 30 minutes

Serves: 4

Preferred spiralizer: Hand-crank

Gluten-free

Good points: This recipe is rich in magnesium and phosphorus, and low in sodium

Nutritional Information Per Serving: Calories: 388;

Total Fat: 16.7g; Saturated Fat: 2.4g; Trans Fat: 0g;

Cholesterol: 100mg; Sodium: 160mg; Potassium: 1185mg;

Total Carbs: 15.6g; Dietary Fiber: 3.7g; Sugar: 4.2g;

Protein: 45.5g; Vitamin A13%; Calcium: 12%;

Vitamin C: 28%; Iron: 13%.

Ingredients:

- 4 salmon filets (approximately 2 lbs.), without skin
- 2 cups of parsnip, spiralized into noodles
- 1 leek stalk, finely sliced
- 1 tablespoon of lemon juice
- 1 small garlic clove, minced
- 2 teaspoons of olive oil
- ¼ teaspoon. of red chili pepper flakes
- ¼ cup of vegetable broth
- 2 teaspoons freshly chopped parsley, to garnish
- Salt and pepper, to taste

Directions:

1. Preheat the oven to 400F.
2. First, make the dressing. Mix 1 tablespoon of olive oil with the lemon juice, and add salt and pepper to taste.
3. Cover a baking tray with baking paper and place the salmon fillets on it. Cover them with the above dressing and place into the oven for 25-30 minutes.
4. As the salmon is cooking, place a skillet over medium heat and add the rest of the olive oil. Put in the parsnip noodles, the leeks and the garlic. Add the red chili pepper flakes and mix them together.
5. Add the vegetable broth in the skillet and let it simmer for 7 to 10 minutes.
6. When the salmon is done cooking, take it out of the tray and place it on a serving dish, near the parsnip pasta.
7. Garnish with fresh parsley and serve immediately.

Asparagus and Spicy Shrimp Over Zoodles

Prep Time: 10 minutes / Cook Time: 10 minutes

Serves: 3

Preferred spiralizer: Hourglass

Vegetarian-friendly

Good points: This recipe is very high in phosphorus and vitamin C, and high in niacin, selenium, vitamin A, vitamin B6, and vitamin B12

Nutritional Information Per Serving: Calories: 283;

Total Fat: 7.9g; Saturated Fat: 1.7g; Trans Fat: 0g;

Cholesterol: 318mg; Sodium: 700mg; Potassium: 950 mg;

Total Carbs: 14.9g; Dietary Fiber: 5g; Sugar: 5.4g;

Protein: 39.8g; Vitamin A: 42%; Calcium: 20%;

Vitamin C: 62%; Iron: 24%

Ingredients:

- 1 pound asparagus, sliced
- 1 pound shrimp, peeled and then deveined
- 2 zucchinis, medium-sized, spiralized into noodles
- 1 tablespoon coconut or olive oil
- 1 teaspoon crushed red pepper
- 1/2 teaspoon sea salt
- 1/4 teaspoon black pepper, fresh ground
- 2 tablespoons lemon juice, fresh squeezed
- 5 garlic cloves, minced
- Fresh parsley, for garnish

Directions:

1. Put the oil in a large-sized, nonstick skillet and heat on medium heat. Add the garlic, asparagus, black pepper, red pepper, and salt. Cook for 2 minutes, frequently stirring.
2. Add the shrimp. Cook for 4 minutes, frequently stirring. Stir in the fresh squeezed lemon juice. When the shrimps are cooked, transfer the mix into a plate. Set aside.
3. Add the zoodles into the same skillet. Sauté for 1 to 2 minutes. Return the shrimp-asparagus mix into the skillet. Gently stir to combine everything. Remove from heat and top with fresh parsley. Serve.

Sautéed Shrimps with Tomato Salsa and Cucumber Spirals

Prep Time: 10 minutes / Cook Time: 10 minutes

Serves: 3

Preferred spiralizer: Hourglass

Gluten-free

Good points: This recipe is rich in vitamins A and C, as well as in phosphorus

Nutritional Information Per Serving: Calories: 246;

Total Fat: 11.4g; Saturated Fat: 1.9g; Trans Fat: 0g;

Cholesterol: 185mg; Sodium: 227mg; Potassium: 849mg;

Total Carbs: 15.2g; Dietary Fiber: 3g; Sugar: 7.7g;

Protein: 22.9g; Vitamin A 41%; Calcium: 14%;

Vitamin C: 48%; Iron: 8%

Ingredients:

- 12 shrimps, peeled
- 2 cucumbers, spiralized
- 4 tomatoes
- 2 tablespoons of olive oil
- 1 tablespoon of red wine vinegar
- ½ cup of fresh basil, chopped
- Salt and pepper to taste

Directions:

1. Start by preparing the salsa. Cut the tomatoes into small dices and place them in a large bowl.
2. Pour 1 tablespoon of olive oil, the red vinegar, the cucumber spirals and the basil and toss well. Season with salt and pepper and set aside.
3. Heat the rest of the olive oil in a skillet over medium heat.
4. Add the shrimps and cook for 2 minutes on each side, until they change color.
5. Transfer the shrimps to the serving plates and add a generous amount of refreshing tomato salsa with cucumber spirals.
6. Serve right away!

Turnip Pasta with Spicy Squid Rings

Prep Time: 10 minutes / Cook Time: 10 minutes

Serves: 2

Preferred spiralizer: Hand-crank

Gluten-free

Good points: This recipe is rich in vitamin C and selenium, as well as being low in sodium

Nutritional Information Per Serving: Calories: 259;

Total Fat: 15.4g; Saturated Fat: 2.4g; Trans Fat: 0g;

Cholesterol: 231mg; Sodium: 139mg; Potassium: 539mg;

Total Carbs: 14.3g; Dietary Fiber: 2.4g; Sugar: 5.5g;

Protein: 17g; Vitamin A 7%; Calcium: 11%;

Vitamin C: 71%; Iron: 7%.

Ingredients

- 7 oz. of squid rings
- 2 turnips, spiralized
- 2 garlic cloves, minced
- ½ cup of basil leaves, chopped
- 1 teaspoon of lime juice
- 1 teaspoon of lime zest
- ½ teaspoon of red chili pepper flakes
- 4 cups of water
- 2 tablespoons of olive oil
- Salt and pepper, to taste

Directions:

1. Heat the water with a pinch of salt in a medium-sized pot and add the turnip pasta. Bring to a boil and cook for 5 minutes. Remove from the heat and set aside.
2. Place a large pan over high heat and add the olive oil.
3. Add the garlic cloves and the squid rings. Stir and cook for 2 minutes.
4. Add the basil leaves, the chili pepper flakes and the lime zest.
5. Season with salt, pepper, and cook for another 2 minutes.
6. Remove the mixture from the heat and transfer it to a serving dish over the turnip pasta. Pour over the lime juice and serve immediately.

Grilled Sea Bass with Zucchini Noodles

Prep Time: 100 minutes / Cook Time: 10 minutes

Serves: 4

Preferred spiralizer: Hourglass

Gluten-free, Vegetarian-friendly

Good points: This recipe is rich in vitamin C and selenium, as well as being low in sodium and sugar

Nutritional Information Per Serving: Calories: 389;

Total Fat: 28.2g; Saturated Fat: 4.4g; Trans Fat: 0g;

Cholesterol: 54mg; Sodium: 105mg; Potassium: 671mg;

Total Carbs: 5.3g; Dietary Fiber: 1.5g; Sugar: 2.5g;

Protein: 25.4g; Vitamin A 16%; Calcium: 4%;

Vitamin C: 54%; Iron: 6%.

Ingredients:

- 4 sea bass fillets
- 2 zucchinis, spiralized
- ½ cup of olive oil
- ¼ cup of freshly squeezed lemon juice
- ½ cup of dry white wine
- ¼ cup of fresh basil, chopped
- ¼ cup of fresh parsley, chopped
- 4 lemon wedges
- Salt and pepper

Directions:

1. Start by preparing the marinade. In a large bowl, mix the olive oil with the lemon juice and the white wine. Add the basil and the parsley, and season with salt and pepper.
2. Take the sea bass fillets and submerge them into the marinade. Cover the bowl with plastic wrap and place it into the refrigerator for 90 minutes.
3. Heat a grill pan and spray it with olive oil.
4. Remove the fish fillets from the marinade and place them on the grill. Do not attempt to turn them for at least 3-4 minutes, otherwise they will break! Use a large spatula to turn the fish and cook it for the same amount of time on the other side.
5. In the meantime, heat some olive oil into a small saucepan. Once hot, pour the zucchini noodles in and sprinkle them with salt and pepper. Cook for 3 minutes.

6. Take the sea bass from the grill and add them to the serving plate next to the zucchinis.
7. Squeeze the lemon wedges over, for a more intense taste. Enjoy!

Shrimps in Coconut Crust with Asparagus and Turnip Noodles

Prep Time: 10 minutes / Cook Time: 15 minutes

Serves: 3

Preferred spiralizer: Hand-crank

Gluten-free

Good points: This recipe is rich in vitamins B6 and C, as well as in iron and selenium

Nutritional Information Per Serving: Calories: 233;

Total Fat: 17.1g; Saturated Fat: 6.3g; Trans Fat: 0g;

Cholesterol: 148mg; Sodium: 153mg; Potassium: 461mg;

Total Carbs: 11.8g; Dietary Fiber: 4.4g; Sugar: 6.2g;

Protein: 11g; Vitamin A 18%; Calcium: 9%;

Vitamin C: 42%; Iron: 26%

Ingredients:

- 10 large shrimps
- ½ cup of coconut flakes
- 2 large eggs, beaten
- ¼ teaspoon of chili flakes
- 2 tablespoons of olive oil
- 2 turnips, spiralized
- 1 tablespoon of lime juice
- 2 cups of asparagus sticks
- 4 cups of water
- Salt and pepper to taste

Directions:

1. Heat slightly salted water into a small pot over medium heat.

2. Carefully peel the shrimps and set aside.
3. In a small bowl, mix the coconut flakes with the chili flakes, salt and pepper.
4. Heat the oil in a large pan over medium heat.
5. Take each shrimp and coat it in the beaten egg before transferring it to the bowl of dry ingredients. When it is well coated with both mixtures, place it into the oil and cook for 3 minutes on each side.
6. In the meantime, add the asparagus and the turnip noodles to the boiling water and cook for 5-7 minutes.
7. Remove the asparagus and the turnips and transfer to the serving dishes.
8. Take the shrimps out and place them by the asparagus and the turnips. Drizzle over the lime juice and serve immediately.

Zucchini Pasta with Smoked Salmon and Peas

Prep Time: 10 minutes / Cook Time: 15 minutes

Serves: 2

Preferred spiralizer: Hourglass

Gluten-free

Good points: This recipe is rich in vitamins B6, B12 and C, and it has low cholesterol

Nutritional Information Per Serving: Calories: 205;

Total Fat: 10.7g; Saturated Fat: 1.8g; Trans Fat: 0g;

Cholesterol: 14mg; Sodium: 1425mg; Potassium: 570mg;

Total Carbs: 12.9g; Dietary Fiber: 4.2g; Sugar: 5.8g;

Protein: 15.8g; Vitamin A 17%; Calcium: 7%;

Vitamin C: 58%; Iron: 11%.

Ingredients:

- 1 large zucchini, spiralized
- 4 oz. smoked salmon
- ½ cup of boiled green peas
- 1 tablespoon olive oil
- ½ cup of red onion, minced
- 2 tablespoons of Dijon mustard

- ¼ cup of vegetable broth
- 1 tablespoon of Greek yogurt
- ½ cup of fresh basil
- Salt and pepper, to taste

Directions:

1. Place a skillet over medium heat and add the olive oil. Once it heats up, add the onion and cook for 3 minutes.
2. Next, add the basil and vegetable broth and bring it to a boil, before letting it simmer on lower heat for around 5 minutes.
3. Add in the Dijon mustard, the Greek yogurt and stir it all together. Season the mixture with salt and pepper.
4. Place the zucchini noodles, the tuna and the peas into the skillet and combine them.
5. Remove the pan from the heat and pour the mixture onto a serving plate.

Salmon Primavera

Prep Time: 10 minutes / Cook Time: 15 minutes

Serves: 3

Preferred spiralizer: Hourglass

Vegetarian-friendly

Good points: This recipe is very high in magnesium, phosphorus, and selenium, high in vitamin C, and low in sugar

Nutritional Information Per Serving: Calories: 393;

Total Fat: 25.2g; Saturated Fat: 3.6g; Trans Fat: 0g;

Cholesterol: 67mg; Sodium: 930 mg; Potassium: 1059mg;

Total Carbs: 11.3g; Dietary Fiber: 5.7g; Sugar: 2.5g;

Protein: 33.3g; Vitamin A: 8%; Calcium: 9%;

Vitamin C: 47%; Iron: 11%

Ingredients:

- 2 zucchinis, medium-sized, spiralized

- 1 bag (10 ounces) frozen California vegetables
- 1 pound salmon, cut into 1-inch pieces)
- 1 teaspoon sea salt, divided
- 1/2 lemon, juice only
- 2 teaspoons dried Herbs de Provence
- 3 tablespoons olive oil, extra-virgin, divided

Directions:

1. Spiralize the zucchini and put into a large-sized bowl. Toss with 1 tablespoon of olive oil and set aside.
2. Remove the skin from the salmon and cut into cubes. Set aside.
3. Juice the lemon half and set aside.
4. Put the remaining 2 tablespoons of olive oil in a large-sized skillet and heat over medium heat. Sprinkle with the Herbs de Provence and stir for about 1 minute until fragrant.
5. Add the frozen California vegetables and toss to coat with the herbed oil. Cover the pan and cook for 5 minutes.
6. Push the vegetables to one side of the skillet. Add the salmon cubes in the cleared area, arranging in a single layer, if possible. Sprinkle the salmon with 1/2 teaspoon of sea salt. Cover the pan and cook for 3 minutes.
7. Flip the salmon, cover the pan again, and cook for 3 minutes.
8. Put the zoodles on top of the veggies and salmon, and sprinkle with the remaining 1/2 teaspoon of sea salt. Cover the pan and cook for another 3 minutes.
9. Add the lemon juice and toss to blend. Serve.

Zucchini Noodles with Shrimp and Bacon

Prep Time: 10 minutes / Cook Time: 15 minutes

Serves: 2

Preferred spiralizer: Hourglass

Gluten-free

Good points: This recipe is rich in vitamins A, B6 and C, as well as in niacin and selenium

Nutritional Information Per Serving: Calories: 399;

Total Fat: 18.6g; Saturated Fat: 6.1g; Trans Fat: 0g;

Cholesterol: 273mg; Sodium: 1182mg; Potassium: 1105mg;

Total Carbs: 14.6g; Dietary Fiber: 3.8g; Sugar: 5.8g;

Protein: 42.8g; Vitamin A 44%; Calcium: 17%;

Vitamin C: 120%; Iron: 15%.

Ingredients:

- 2 zucchinis, peeled and spiralized
- 10 shrimps, shells removed
- 4 slices of bacon
- 1 garlic clove, minced
- ½ teaspoon of red pepper flakes
- 1 small red onion
- 1 teaspoon of lemon zest
- 4 tablespoons of lemon juice
- ½ cup chopped parsley
- Salt and pepper, to taste

Directions:

1. Place a skillet over medium heat. Cook the bacon into the heated oil for 5 minutes. Remove and set aside.
2. In the same resulting oil, add the garlic, the onion, the red pepper flakes and the shrimps. Cook the shrimp for 2 or 3 minutes, while pouring the lemon juice and zest over the shrimp. Sprinkle salt and pepper to taste.
3. Remove the shrimp and set aside.
4. In the remaining mixture of onion and garlic, place the zucchini noodles and cook for a few minutes. Add the bacon and the shrimp and toss to mix it together.
5. Remove from the heat, garnish with the chopped parsley and serve.

Pesto Salmon and Zoodles

Prep Time: 15 minutes / Cook Time: 20 minutes

Serves: 2

Preferred spiralizer: Hourglass

Vegetarian-friendly

Good points: This recipe is very high in phosphorus and high in magnesium and selenium

Nutritional Information Per Serving: Calories: 799;

Total Fat: 63.3g; Saturated Fat: 11.6g; Trans Fat: 0g;

Cholesterol: 108mg; Sodium: 850mg; Potassium: mg;

Total Carbs: g; Dietary Fiber: g; Sugar: 1047g;

Protein: 10.9g; Vitamin A: 31%; Calcium: 48%;

Vitamin C: 38%; Iron: 13%

Ingredients:

- 1 cup pesto
- 1 zucchini
- 2 salmon fillets
- Large handful grape or cherry tomatoes

Directions:

1. Preheat the oven to 400F.
2. Place 1 piece salmon in a piece tin foil and a few pieces of grape or cherry tomatoes. Spread a couple tablespoons pesto over the top of the salmon. Seal the foil into a packet around the tomatoes and salmon. Repeat the process with the remaining salmon, tomatoes, and pesto.
3. Bake for about 20 minutes or until the salmon easily flakes when tested with a fork.
4. While the salmon fillets are cooking, spiralize the zucchini and cook lightly in a skillet or pan on medium heat along with some more tomatoes. After 3 minutes, a spoonful pesto at a time, add pesto until the zoodles are coated lightly. Cook for1-2 minutes more. Divide between 2 bowls.
5. Unwrap the foil packets and put the salmon and tomatoes on top of each zoodle serving.

VEGETARIAN

Shredded Kale, Brussels Sprouts, and Pear Noodle

Prep Time: 22 minutes / Cook Time: 5 minutes

Serves: 4

Preferred spiralizer: Hourglass

Vegetarian-friendly

Good points: This recipe is very high in vitamin A and vitamin C, high in manganese, low in sodium, and has no cholesterol

Nutritional Information Per Serving: Calories: 157;

Total Fat: 11g; Saturated Fat: 1g; Trans Fat: 0g;

Cholesterol: 0mg; Sodium: 34mg; Potassium: 350mg;

Total Carbs: 15g; Dietary Fiber: 4g; Sugar: 7g;

Protein: 4g; Vitamin A: 40%; Calcium: 6%;

Vitamin 97C: %; 7Iron: %

Ingredients:

For the vinaigrette:

- 1 tablespoon shallot, minced
- 1 teaspoon honey
- 1/2 teaspoon Dijon mustard
- 2 tablespoons apple cider vinegar
- 2 tablespoons olive oil, extra virgin
- Salt and pepper, to taste

For the salad:

- 1 cup kale, shredded or finely chopped
- 1 pear (Anjou or Bosc), spiralized using Blade D into noodles
- 3 tablespoons blanched almonds, sliced
- 6 ounces (about 2 cups) Brussels sprouts, thinly sliced

Directions:

1. Put a medium-sized skillet on medium-high heat. When the skillet is heated, add the sliced almonds and cook, frequently shaking the pan for about 3 minutes or until fragrant and toasted. Set aside.
2. In a bowl, whisk all the dressing ingredients until combined. Taste and adjust to your preference.
3. In a large-sized mixing bowl, combine and toss the pear noodles with the kale, toasted almonds, and Brussels sprouts. Drizzle with the vinaigrette. Toss again and serve.

Cold Spiralized Sesame Noodle

Prep Time: 35 minutes / Cook Time: 0 minutes

Serves: 4

Preferred spiralizer: Hourglass

Vegetarian-friendly

Good points: This recipe is very high in vitamin A, high in manganese, magnesium, and vitamin C, and has no cholesterol

Nutritional Information Per Serving: Calories: 255;

Total Fat: 19g; Saturated Fat: 2g; Trans Fat: 0g;

Cholesterol: 0mg; Sodium: 508mg; Potassium: 572mg;

Total Carbs: 14g; Dietary Fiber: 4g; Sugar: 5g;

Protein: 10g; Vitamin A: 98%; Calcium: 14%;

Vitamin C: 46%; Iron: 18%

Ingredients:

- 1 carrot, large-sized, peeled, spiralized into noodles using Blade D and trimmed to shorter strands
- 1 English cucumber, seedless, spiralized into noodles using Blade D and trimmed to shorter strands
- 1 zucchini, medium-sized, spiralized into noodles using Blade D and trimmed to shorter strands
- 1/2 cup almonds, roasted unsalted, roughly chopped
- 1/2 cup shelled frozen edamame, and defrosted, OR peas
- 4-5 cups spinach, thinly sliced

For the dressing:

- 1 garlic clove, pressed and then minced
- 1 tablespoon ginger, freshly grated
- 1 tablespoons sesame oil
- 1 tablespoons sesame seeds
- 1 teaspoon honey
- 1 teaspoon of red pepper flakes OR chili garlic sauce
- 1/4 cup rice vinegar
- 2 tablespoons tahini or creamy almond butter
- 2 tablespoons tamari OR soy sauce

Directions:

1. Pat the cucumber noodles with a clean kitchen towel or paper towels to remove excess moisture and put the zoodles in a large-sized mixing bowl. Add the zucchini noodles or carrot. Add the almonds, spinach, and edamame.
2. In a bowl, whisk all the dressing ingredients together until creamy. Taste and adjust, if needed.
3. Pour the dressing over the noodles. Toss thoroughly until combined. Serve immediately.
4. If not serving immediately, chill in the refrigerator for 1-2 days.

Broccoli, Pesto Turnip Rice, and Poached Egg

Prep Time: 20 minutes / Cook Time: 15 minutes

Serves: 3

Preferred spiralizer: Hourglass

Vegetarian-friendly

Good points: This recipe is

Nutritional Information Per Serving: Calories:

Total Fat: g; Saturated Fat: g; Trans Fat: 0g;

Cholesterol: mg; Sodium: mg; Potassium: mg;

Total Carbs: g; Dietary Fiber: g; Sugar: g;

Protein: g; Vitamin A: %; Calcium: %;

Vitamin C: %; Iron: %

Ingredients:

- 3 large eggs
- 2 1/2 cups broccoli florets, small-sized
- 2 turnips, large-sized, peeled, and spiralized using Blade C
- 1 tablespoon extra-virgin olive oil
- 1 pinch red pepper flakes
- 1 garlic clove, large-sized, minced
- Salt and pepper, to taste

For the pesto:

- 1 1/2 cups basil leaves, packed
- 1 clove garlic, large-sized, minced
- 1 tablespoon parmesan cheese, grated
- 1/2 teaspoon sea salt, grinded
- 1/4 cup olive oil
- 1/4 teaspoon pepper, grinded
- 2 tablespoons pine nuts

Directions:

1. Fill a medium-sized saucepan half full with water and bring to a boil. When the water is boiling, add the broccoli. Cook for 2 to 3 minutes or until the florets are more easily pierced with a fork. Drain in a colander and thoroughly pat dry. Set aside.
2. While waiting for the broccoli florets to cook, put the turnip noodles into a food processor; pulse until the consistency is like rice. Set aside. Wipe the food processor and set aside until needed.
3. Heat a large-sized skillet over medium heat. Add the olive oil. When hot, add the garlic and red pepper flakes and cook for 30 seconds or until fragrant. Add the broccoli and turnip rice. Season with pepper and salt, cover, and cook for 5 minutes or until the turnip rice is soft like rice.
4. While the turnips are cooking, put all the pesto ingredients into the food processor; pulse until the mixture is creamy. Taste and adjust to your taste.
5. When the turnips are cooked, transfer the turnip rice mixture into a large-sized mixing bowl. Add the pesto and toss to combine. Set aside.

6. After the pesto rice is assembled, fill a medium-sized saucepan half full with water; bring to steady simmer. Crack an egg into individual small-sized bowl or ramekin. Create a gentle whirlpool in the simmering water – this will help the egg white around the egg yolk. Slowly dip the egg in the water and cook for 3 minutes. Using a slotted spoon, remove from water and gently put in a plate lined with a paper towel to drain.
7. Divide the turnip pesto mixture between plates and top each serving with poached egg. Serve right away.

Spiralized Root Vegetable

Prep Time: 20 minutes, plus chilling/ Cook Time: 0 minutes

Serves: 4-6

Preferred spiralizer: Hourglass

Vegetarian-friendly

Good points: This recipe is very high in vitamin A, high in vitamin C, and very low in cholesterol

Nutritional Information Per Serving: Calories: 147;

Total Fat: 11.5g; Saturated Fat: 1.8g; Trans Fat: 0g;

Cholesterol: 0mg; Sodium: 80mg; Potassium: 277mg;

Total Carbs: 9.9g; Dietary Fiber: 2.9g; Sugar: 2.9g;

Protein: 3g; Vitamin A: 106%; Calcium: 4%;

Vitamin C: 16%; Iron: 7%

Ingredients:

- 3 carrots, multicolored peeled
- 1/2 celery root, peeled
- 1 parsnip, medium-sized, peeled
- 2 tablespoons pumpkin seeds, roasted, roughly chopped
- 2 tablespoons pistachios, roasted, roughly chopped
- 2 tablespoons parsley, roughly chopped, PLUS more for garnish
- 2 tablespoons mint, roughly chopped, PLUS more for garnish
- 2 tablespoons lemon juice
- 2 tablespoons Greek yogurt, plain

- 1/4 cup olive oil
- 1/4 cup hummus
- Kosher salt and freshly ground black pepper, to taste

Directions:

1. With the smallest blade of a spiralizer, spiralize the carrots, celery root, and parsnips. Transfer into a medium-sized bowl and cover with ice water. If using purple-colored carrot, spiralizer it last and put into a different bowl to prevent the color from bleeding. Let sit for at least 15 minutes or until the vegetables are firm. Drain the veggies and dry well using a salad spinner.
2. In a large-sized bowl, whisk the olive oil and lemon juice. Add the veggies and herbs; toss to coat. Season with pepper and salt.
3. In a small-sized bowl, season the yogurt with pepper and salt. With the back of a large-sized spoor, smear the hummus on one side of a serving platter. Pile the salad high in the center of the platter. Garnish with a dollop of the seasoned yogurt, the pistachios, pumpkin seeds, parsley, and mint. Serve.

Honey Mustard Zoodles

Prep Time: 5 minutes / Cook Time: 3 minutes

Serves: 2

Preferred spiralizer: Hourglass

Vegetarian-friendly

Good points: This recipe is very high in vitamin B6 and vitamin C, high in vitamin A, and very low in cholesterol

Nutritional Information Per Serving: Calories: 139;

Total Fat: 9.2g; Saturated Fat: 1.2g; Trans Fat: 0g;

Cholesterol: 3mg; Sodium: 79mg; Potassium: 313mg;

Total Carbs: 13.9g; Dietary Fiber: 1.8g; Sugar: 9.2g;

Protein: 2.8g; Vitamin A: 16%; Calcium: 3%;

Vitamin C: 84%; Iron: 8%

Ingredients:

- 1 zucchini
- 1 cup mushrooms
- 1 tablespoon honey
- 1 tablespoon mustard
- 1 tablespoon olive oil
- 1/2 red bell pepper, diced
- 2 tablespoons mayo

Directions:

1. Spiralize the zucchini into noodles.
2. In a rimmed cookie sheet, toss the mushrooms and bell pepper with the olive oil. Broil until the veggies are soft.
3. In a small-sized, mix the honey, mustard, and mayo.
4. In a skillet on medium heat, add the zucchini and 1 tablespoon water. Sauté for about 3 minutes or until the zoodles are soft. If needed, add more water.
5. Add the broiled veggies and the honey mix. Toss to coat.

Baked Parsnip Noodles with Cauliflower and Cheese Casserole

Prep Time: 10 minutes / Cook Time: 50 minutes

Serves: 6

Preferred spiralizer: Hand-crank

Good points: This recipe is rich in vitamins B6 and C

Nutritional Information Per Serving: Calories: 373;

Total Fat: 25.8g; Saturated Fat: 15.3g; Trans Fat: 0g;

Cholesterol: 223mg; Sodium: 344mg; Potassium: 573mg;

Total Carbs: 21g; Dietary Fiber: 5g; Sugar: 8g;

Protein: 16.2g; Vitamin A 17%; Calcium: 34%;

Vitamin C: 70%; Iron: 7%.

Ingredients:

- 1 head (400 grams) cauliflower, cut into florets
- 2 cups of parsnips, spiralized
- 3 egg yolks

- 3 egg whites
- ¼ cup of butter
- 1 tablespoon of white flour
- 1 cup of milk
- 1 cup of Cheddar cheese, shredded
- Salt and pepper, to taste

Directions:

1. Preheat the oven to 400F. Place the cauliflower florets in a medium-sized pot and cover with water. Place over high heat and bring to a boil. Cook for 10 minutes before draining the florets and setting them aside.
2. Heat the butter in a medium-sized skillet. Add the flour and stir continuously for 2 minutes. Pour in the milk and bring to a boil.
3. Remove from the heat and add half of the breadcrumbs, the egg yolks, the cheese, salt and pepper. Mix well, and add the cauliflower, as well.
4. In a small bowl, whisk the egg whites until they are stiff.
5. Mix the 2 compositions and pour them into a baking tray.
6. Sprinkle the parsnip noodles and the remaining breadcrumbs on top and place the tray into the oven. Bake for 30-35 minutes.
7. Remove from the oven and serve immediately.

Cashew Satay Spiralized Vegetable Stir Fry

Prep Time: 12 minutes / Cook Time: 6 minutes

Serves:

Preferred spiralizer: Hourglass

Vegetarian-friendly

Good points: This recipe is very high in vitamin A and vitamin C, high in manganese, magnesium, potassium, riboflavin, and vitamin B6, and has no cholesterol

Nutritional Information Per Serving: Calories: 146;

Total Fat: 9g; Saturated Fat: 1.5g; Trans Fat: 0g;

Cholesterol: 0 mg; Sodium: 785 mg; Potassium: 680mg;

Total Carbs: 14.2g; Dietary Fiber: 3.2g; Sugar: 6.7g;

Protein: 5.6g; Vitamin A: 34%; Calcium: %7;

Vitamin C: 76%; Iron: 10%

Ingredients:

- 2-3 yellow squash and/or zucchini, spiralized to noodles
- 2-3 tablespoon creamy cashew butter, OR tahini - just adjust according to how much zucchini you use
- 2 tablespoon tamaris OR any gluten-free soy sauce
- 2 handfuls Napa cabbage, chopped, or more if you want more veggies
- 1/4 teaspoon five spice Asian seasoning
- 1/2-1 teaspoon red chili flakes
- 1 teaspoon garlic, minced
- 1 teaspoon agave nectar OR honey if you're not vegan
- 1 tablespoon sesame oil
- 1 shallot OR 2-3 tablespoons red onion, chopped
- 1 dash sea salt
- Black pepper, to taste

Directions:

1. Spiralize the squash and the zucchini, and then clean and dry. Chop your red onion and cabbage.
2. Heat a skillet or a wok to medium high or high. Add the cashew butter – make sure it's creamy or melted and smooth. Add the chili flakes, garlic, tamari, and sesame oil. Mix all together.
3. Toss the vegetables, the rest of the ingredients, spices, and seasonings in the skillet.
4. Stir-fry for a couple of minutes or until the vegetables are coated and cooked, but not soggy.
5. Remove from heat and, if desired, garnish with more black pepper and chili flakes.

Notes: If you want meat, serve with cooked shrimp, beef, or chicken.

Spiralized Beets and Goat Cheese Winter Kale Bowl

Prep Time: 15 minutes / Cook Time: 6 minutes

Serves: 2

Preferred spiralizer: Hourglass

Vegetarian-friendly

Good points: This recipe is very high in vitamin A and vitamin C, high in manganese, and low in cholesterol and sodium

Nutritional Information Per Serving: Calories: 266;

Total Fat: 20.6g; Saturated Fat: 5.5g; Trans Fat: 0g;

Cholesterol: 15mg; Sodium: 104mg; Potassium: 472mg;

Total Carbs: 14.8g; Dietary Fiber: 2.1g; Sugar: 5.8g;

Protein: 8.2g; Vitamin A: 211%; Calcium: 23%;

Vitamin C: 137%; Iron: 10%

Ingredients:

- 1 beet, large-sized, peeled, and spiralized into noodles using Blade D, noodles trimmed to shorter strands
- 3cups kale, chopped
- 3 tablespoons goat cheese, crumbled
- 2 tablespoons walnuts, chopped
- 2 tablespoons pomegranate arils
- 2 tablespoons PLUS 2 teaspoons extra-virgin olive oil
- 1 teaspoon honey
- 1 1/2 tablespoons apple cider vinegar
- Salt and pepper

Directions:

1. Preheat the oven to 425F.
2. Line a baking sheet with parchment paper. Lay out the beet noodles on the baking sheet. Drizzle with 2 teaspoons of olive oil and season with pepper and salt. Toast to coat the beet noodles with the oil. Roast in the oven for about 6 to 8 minutes or, if you want a softer noodle, longer.
3. Meanwhile, put the olive oil, honey, apple cider vinegar, pepper, and salt in a large-sized mixing bowl. Whisk to combine. Add the kale. Using tongs, massage the kale for about 30 seconds to 1 minutes to soften.
4. When the beets are roasted, divide between 2 bowls. Top with the beet noodles, walnuts, goat cheese, and pomegranates. Serve.

Eggs in Root Vegetable Baskets

Prep Time: 15 minutes / Cook Time: 21-22 minutes

Serves: 6

Preferred spiralizer: Hourglass

Vegetarian-friendly

Good points: This recipe is very high in vitamin B6, and high in selenium and vitamin C

Nutritional Information Per Serving: Calories: 161;

Total Fat: 9.7g; Saturated Fat: 2.2g; Trans Fat: 0g;

Cholesterol: 186mg; Sodium: 119mg; Potassium: 353mg;

Total Carbs: 11.6g; Dietary Fiber: 1.8g; Sugar: 3.4g;

Protein: 7.5g; Vitamin A: 7%; Calcium: 3%;

Vitamin C: 23%; Iron: 11%

Ingredients:

- 1 beet, large-sized, peeled
- 1 Russet potato, large-sized, peeled
- 1 sweet potato, large-sized, peeled
- 2 tablespoons olive oil
- 6 eggs, large-sized
- Sprinkle salt and pepper

Directions:

1. Preheat the oven to 400F.
2. Using the thin setting, spiralizer the vegetables into spaghetti noodles.
3. Toss the veggies with the olive oil and press them into 6 pieces large-sized muffin tins. You can use 1 cup-sized ramekins. Bake for 20 minutes. Frequently check every 2 minutes or until the veggies are cooked to your liking, preferably al dente since they will cook more with the added eggs.
4. Remove from the oven and crack 1 egg into the well of each muffin tin. Bake for 1-2 minute more. Run a knife around the edges of each baked egg bundle. Carefully remove and set on serving plates. Serve immediately.

Smoky Summer Vegetable Tangle

Prep Time: minutes / Cook Time: minutes

Serves: 4-6

Preferred spiralizer: Hourglass

Vegetarian-friendly

Good points: This recipe is very high in vitamin A and vitamin C, high in fiber, potassium, riboflavin, selenium, and vitamin B6, and has no cholesterol

Nutritional Information Per Serving: Calories: 183;

Total Fat: 13g; Saturated Fat: 3.8g; Trans Fat: 0g;

Cholesterol: 0mg; Sodium: 224mg; Potassium: 732mg;

Total Carbs: 14.4g; Dietary Fiber: 5g; Sugar: 4.5g;

Protein: 6g; Vitamin A: 88%; Calcium: 7%;

Vitamin C: 51%; Iron: 10%

Ingredients:

For the smoky sauce:

- 2-3 garlic cloves, minced
- 2 tablespoons olive oil
- 2 tablespoons Dijon mustard
- 1/4 teaspoon sriracha OR your choice of hot sauce
- 1 teaspoon tamari
- 1 tablespoon smoked paprika
- 1 lemon, juice only

For the tangle:

- 1 carrot, medium-sized, shaved into ribbons using a vegetable peeler
- 1-2 firm zucchini, small to medium-sized, spiralized into noodles
- 1/2 tablespoon PLUS 1 teaspoon neutral coconut oil, divided
- 1/2-pound cremini mushrooms, sliced
- 1/2 lemon, juice only
- 1 shallot, chopped

- 2 large-sized handfuls young green beans, strings removed if present
- Few tablespoons almonds or hazelnuts, chopped, toasted if preferred
- Handful parsley leaves, chopped, optional
- Microgreens and/or salad greens
- Tamari, for drizzling, to taste

Directions:

1. In a small-sized bowl, combine all the smoky sauce ingredients using a whisk until smooth. Set aside.
2. In a platter or in a large-sized mixing bowl, combine the carrots and zucchini. Set aside.
3. Put 1/2 tablespoon of coconut oil in a large-sized sauté pan and heat over medium heat. Add shallot; sauté for 5 minutes.
4. Add the mushrooms; sauté for about 5 to 7 minutes or until they start to brown. Drizzle lightly with tamari and stir to until absorbed. Put the sautéed mushroom mix into the platter/bowl of carrots and zucchini.
5. In the same saucepan, put 1 teaspoon of coconut oil and warm over medium heat. Add the green beans and sauté for about 2 to 3 minutes or until blistered in some places and bright green.
6. Squeeze lemon juice over the beans and drizzle lightly with tamari. Add into the platter/bowl with veggies.
7. Add the parsley and, if using, microgreens and/or salad greens. Drizzle with the smoky sauce over the vegetables. Toss to coat and then sprinkle with the chopped nuts. Serve immediately.

Notes: Store leftovers in the refrigerator for up to 3 days – the vegetables will become marinated and taste delicious in a new way.

Grilled Tomatoes and Zucchini Noodles

Prep Time: 10 minutes / Cook Time: 15 minutes

Serves: 4

Preferred spiralizer: Hourglass

Gluten-free, Paleo-friendly

Good points: This recipe is very high in vitamin A and riboflavin and in dietary fiber

Nutritional Information Per Serving: Calories: 119;

Total Fat: 7.6g; Saturated Fat: 1.1g; Trans Fat: 0g;

Cholesterol: 0mg; Sodium: 27mg; Potassium: 852mg;

Total Carbs: 12.1g; Dietary Fiber: 3.8g; Sugar: 7g;

Protein: 3.6g; Vitamin A 32%; Calcium: 5%;

Vitamin C: 87%; Iron: 6%.

Ingredients:

- 4 medium-sized zucchinis, spiralized
- 3 large tomatoes, sliced
- ¼ cup of balsamic vinegar
- 2 tablespoons of olive oil
- 2 tablespoons. of basil, freshly chopped
- Salt and pepper, to taste

Directions:

1. Place a grill over high heat.
2. Drizzle olive oil over the zucchinis and the tomatoes and season them with salt and pepper.
3. Add them in batches on the grill and cook on each side for 2-3 minutes. Be careful not to burn them!
4. Place the grilled tomatoes and the zucchinis in a large bowl and toss.
5. Pour over the balsamic vinegar and sprinkle the chopped basil. Serve right away!

Cauliflower Alfredo Zoodles with Spring Vegetables and Asparagus

Prep Time: 15 minutes / Cook Time: 13 minutes

Serves: 8

Preferred spiralizer: Hourglass

Vegetarian-friendly

Good points: This recipe is very high in fiber, manganese, pantothenic acid, phosphorus, potassium, riboflavin, thiamin, vitamin A, vitamin B6, and vitamin C, high in iron and magnesium, and low in saturated fat and sodium, and has no cholesterol

Nutritional Information Per Serving: Calories: 79;

Total Fat: 0.7g; Saturated Fat: 0g; Trans Fat: 0g;

Cholesterol: 0 mg; Sodium: 35mg; Potassium: 680mg;

Total Carbs: 15.4g; Dietary Fiber: 4.8g; Sugar: 3.9g;

Protein: 6.3g; Vitamin A: 22%; Calcium: 7%;

Vitamin C: 94%; Iron: 13%

Ingredients:

Roasted garlic cauliflower alfredo sauce:

- 5-6 cups cauliflower florets OR 1 large-sized head cauliflower
- 5 garlic heads, roasted
- 1/8 teaspoon cayenne pepper, optional
- 1/4 cup nutritional yeast
- 1/2 cup reserved cooking water from cooking the cauliflower
- 1 teaspoon smoked paprika
- 1 teaspoon fresh squeezed key lime OR lime juice
- Salt and black pepper, to taste

For the zucchini noodles:

- 5 zucchinis, medium-sized, spiralized into noodles
- 1 - 1 1/2 cups mix of broccoli florets, shredded carrots, Brussels sprouts, cherry tomatoes, and red pepper
- 2 cloves garlic, minced
- 1/2 bunch asparagus, trimmed and cut into 3/4-inch pieces
- 1 -2 teaspoon nutritional yeast, for sprinkling, optional
- Fresh parsley, chopped

Directions:

1. Spiralize the zucchini using the ribbon blade of your spiralizer. Set aside. Using a paper towel, dry the zoodles.

2. Put the cauliflower florets into a large-sized pot and cover with water. Bring to a boil over medium-high heat and then lower the heat to medium. Cook for 6 to 8 minutes or until fork tender.
3. With a slotted spoon, transfer the cooked cauliflower into a blender. Add the roasted garlic, nutritional yeast, and smoked paprika. Blend. Add 2 to 3 tablespoons of the reserved cooking liquid and continue blending until the mixture is smooth.
4. Add more water as needed to thin out the sauce while blending the sauce. Season with black pepper, salt, and cayenne pepper, if desired.
5. Put the olive oil in a large-sized skillet and heat over medium heat. Add the garlic and cook for 30 seconds or until fragrant.
6. Add the asparagus and the other vegetables; sauté for about 3 to 4 minutes or until tender.
7. Add the zucchini; cook for 1 to 2 minutes or just soft –DO NOT OVERCOOK.
8. Add the sauce into the skillet and toss well to coat. Season to taste and then sprinkle with parsley, and if desired, with nutritional yeast. Serve immediately.

VEGAN

Carrot Noodles with Tofu Cheese

Prep Time: 10 minutes / Cook Time: 20 minutes

Serves: 2

Preferred spiralizer: Hourglass

Gluten-free

Good points: This recipe is very high in vitamin A and has no cholesterol

Nutritional Information Per Serving: Calories: 218;

Total Fat: 16.4g; Saturated Fat: 12.4g; Trans Fat: 0g;

Cholesterol: 0mg; Sodium: 84mg; Potassium: 488mg;

Total Carbs: 14.3g; Dietary Fiber: 3.6g; Sugar: 5.9g;

Protein: 6.4g; Vitamin A 368%; Calcium: 17%;

Vitamin C: 12%; Iron: 9%.

Ingredients:

- 2 cups of carrots, peeled and spiralized
- 1 tablespoon of ginger, minced
- 1 garlic clove, minced
- 2 tablespoons of coconut oil
- ½ cup of vegan feta tofu cheese, diced
- Salt and pepper, to taste

Directions:

1. Place a saucepan over medium heat. Add one tablespoon of the coconut oil and once it heats up, add the garlic and the ginger. Cook for 2 minutes.
2. Add the carrot noodles and season with salt and pepper. Toss well and let it cook for 5 minutes.
3. Take a small grill and place it on high heat. Brush the dices of tofu cheese with coconut oil and place them on the grill. Cook for 1 minute on each side.
4. Take out the carrot noodles and place them on a serving dish.
5. Place the grilled tofu next to it.

Lemon Mushroom Zoodles

Prep Time: 15 minutes / Cook Time: 5 minutes

Serves: 4

Preferred spiralizer: Hourglass

Vegetarian and vegan-friendly and gluten-free

Good points: This recipe is very high in fiber, iron, niacin, pantothenic acid, phosphorus, potassium, riboflavin, selenium, thiamin, vitamin B6, and vitamin C, and high in manganese, magnesium, vitamin A, and zinc, is low in saturated fat and sodium, and has no cholesterol

Nutritional Information Per Serving: Calories: 61;

Total Fat: 1.8g; Saturated Fat: 0g; Trans Fat: 0g;

Cholesterol: 0mg; Sodium: 17mg; Potassium: 705mg;

Total Carbs: 9.7g; Dietary Fiber: 3.3g; Sugar: 4.6g;

Protein: 5.7g; Vitamin A: 9%; Calcium: 3%;

Vitamin C: 49%; Iron: 24%

Ingredients:

- 2 zucchinis, medium-sized, spiralized
- 16 ounces' mushrooms, sliced
- 1 bunch asparagus, ends removed and cut into 2-inch segments
- 1 teaspoon olive oil
- 1 tablespoon water
- 1 lemon, zested ad juice

Directions:

1. Toss the asparagus with olive oil and broil until soft. Set aside.
2. Heat the skillet on the stovetop over medium heat. Add 1 tablespoon of water and then the mushrooms. Stir to heat. Cook for about 1 to 2 minutes.
3. Add the spiralized zucchini and cook for 3 minutes.
4. Add the lemon and zest, and stir to coat.
5. Stir in the asparagus gently in the skillet.

Spicy Sesame Zoodles with Crispy Tofu

Prep Time: minutes / Cook Time: minutes

Serves: 6

Preferred spiralizer: Hourglass

Vegetarian-friendly

Good points: This recipe is very high in vitamin B6, high in manganese and vitamin C, and very low in cholesterol

Nutritional Information Per Serving: Calories: 266;

Total Fat: 19.9g; Saturated Fat: 3.4g; Trans Fat: 0g;

Cholesterol: 1mg; Sodium: 738mg; Potassium: 586mg;

Total Carbs: 14.7g; Dietary Fiber: 3.2g; Sugar: 8.5g;

Protein: 10.3g; Vitamin A: 12%; Calcium: 12%;

Vitamin C: 43%; Iron: 17 %

Ingredients:

For the chili sesame sauce:

- 1/2 cup peanut butter
- 1 clove garlic, minced
- 1 knob fresh ginger, peeled and then grated
- 1/3 cup light soy sauce, low sodium
- 1/3 cup sesame oil
- 1/4 cup rice vinegar
- 2 tablespoons chili paste
- 2 tablespoons sugar

For the zoodle and tofu:

- 4-6 zucchinis
- 12 ounces' tofu extra-firm
- Scallions and sesame seeds, for topping

Directions:

1. Put all if the chili sesame sauce ingredients together and shake to combine. Alternatively, you can put them in a food processor and process to combine. If you are going to serve this cold, chill in the fridge for a while.
2. Press the excess moisture out of the tofu and then cut into bite-sized pieces.
3. Put a tiny bit of oil in a nonstick pan and heat. Add the tofu and stir fry until golden brown. Add about 1/2 cup of sauce and simmer until the sauce begins to evaporate and the tofu absorbs it and becomes browned in the pan.
4. Keep flipping gently and scraping the browned bits off the bottom – you should end up with nicely golden browned tofu cubes and with some yummy browned sauce bits.
5. Spiralize the zucchini and then toss about 1/4 cup of sauce per serving.
6. Top with tofu, scallions, and sesame seeds. Serve immediately.

Notes: Not cooking the zoodles makes this dish into a creamy and cold, salad-like crunchy dish. You can cook the zoodles if you wish. Please note that whether you cook the zoodles or not, they will get a little watery because of the sauce, so serve immediately after tossing. Cook more tofu, if desired, depending on how hungry you are.

Roasted Mushroom and Vegetable Zucchini Noodle Bowls

Prep Time: 15 minutes / Cook Time: 50 minutes

Serves: 6

Preferred spiralizer: Hourglass

Vegetarian-friendly

Good points: This recipe is very high in selenium, vitamin A, and vitamin C, and high in manganese, niacin, phosphorus, potassium, riboflavin, and vitamin B6, and has no cholesterol

Nutritional Information Per Serving: Calories: 193;

Total Fat: 11.9g; Saturated Fat: 1.4g; Trans Fat: 0g;

Cholesterol: 0mg; Sodium: 1525mg; Potassium: 1020mg;

Total Carbs: 14.4g; Dietary Fiber: 2.9g; Sugar: 5.9g;

Protein: 8.5g; Vitamin A: 82%; Calcium: 6%;

Vitamin C: 90%; Iron: 12%

Ingredients:

For the roasted mushrooms:

- 1 1/2 pounds' cremini mushrooms
- 1 teaspoon black pepper, fresh ground
- 1 teaspoon sea salt, fine grain
- 3 tablespoons grapeseed oil

For the noodles:

- 1 pound zucchini
- 1 cup carrots, matchstick-cut (about 3 ounces)
- 1 fresh red chili pepper, minced, optional
- 1 red bell pepper, thinly sliced
- 1 tablespoon grapeseed oil
- 1/4 cup soy sauce (OR gluten-free tamari, soy sauce, or coconut aminos)
- 2 tablespoons fresh ginger, minced
- 2 teaspoons toasted sesame oil
- 3 tablespoons fresh basil, chopped
- 3 tablespoons fresh cilantro, chopped
- 3 tablespoons fresh mint, chopped
- 4 cups vegetable stock
- 4 garlic cloves, minced

Directions:

1. Preheat the oven to 425F. Put the mushrooms in a large-sized bowl. Drizzle with oil and sprinkle with pepper and salt. With your hands, toss everything together. Spread the mushrooms on a rimmed baking sheet. Put in the oven and bake for about 40 minutes or until for tender and browned. Remove from the oven and let cool slightly, then cut into halves or quarters and set aside.
2. Cut the ends off the zucchini, peel them or leave the skin on for extra color, and spiralize into noodles, discarding the center seeded portion, and set aside.
3. Heat a medium-sized saucepan on medium heat. Add the ginger, garlic, and if using, chili pepper. Cook for 1 minute, constantly stirring. Add the vegetable stock and soy sauce, and bring to a boil. When boiling, reduce the heat to medium-low and simmer for 8 minutes.
4. Add the zoodles and return to a simmer, and cook for 2 minutes.

5. Divide the zoodles and broth between serving bowl. Top each with the mushrooms, bell pepper, and carrots. Sprinkle the top of each serving with the herbs and then drizzle with the toasted sesame oil.

Spiralized Ratatouille

Prep Time: 25 minutes / Cook Time: 30 minutes

Serves: 4

Preferred spiralizer: Hourglass

Vegetarian-friendly

Good points: This recipe is very high in vitamin A and vitamin C, is high in fiber, manganese, potassium, and vitamin B6, is low in sodium, and has no cholesterol

Nutritional Information Per Serving: Calories: 102;

Total Fat: 5.3g; Saturated Fat: 0.8g; Trans Fat: 0g;

Cholesterol: 0mg; Sodium: 42 mg; Potassium: 639mg;

Total Carbs: 13.8g; Dietary Fiber: 4.1g; Sugar: 7.9g;

Protein: 2.9g; Vitamin A: 54%; Calcium: 5%;

Vitamin C: 181 %; Iron: 7%

Ingredients:

- 1 can (28 ounces) whole peeled tomatoes, with their juices
- 1 cup julienned eggplant, packed (from 1 small-sized eggplant – you will have leftovers)
- 1 medium yellow squash, spiralized with blade A, spiralized using the blade A into noodles and cut into shorter strands
- 1 medium zucchini, spiralized with blade D, spiralized using the blade A into noodles and cut into shorter strands
- 1 sweet yellow (or Vidalia) onion, peeled, spiralized using the blade A into noodles and cut into shorter strands
- 2 red bell peppers, spiralized with blade A, spiralized using the blade A into noodles and cut into shorter strands
- 1 bay leaf
- 1 tablespoon fresh oregano OR 1 teaspoon dried oregano
- 1/4 cup packed fresh basil, finely chopped

- 1/4 teaspoon red pepper flakes
- 2 large garlic cloves, pressed or minced
- 2 tablespoons olive oil
- Freshly ground black pepper
- Salt

Directions:

1. In a Dutch oven or a large-sized pot, put the oil and heat over medium heat or until shimmering. Add the garlic, onion, red pepper flakes. Cook, frequently stirring, for about 5 minutes or until the onion is soft.
2. Add the eggplant, squash noodles, zucchini, and bell pepper. Season with pepper and salt. Cook for about 7-10 minutes or until the veggies are soft.
3. Over the pot – be aware of the red splashes –individually crush the tomatoes using your hands and then add each one into the pot and add the tomato juices as well.
4. Stir in the oregano and bay leaf. Increase the heat to high and bring the mix to a boil and then reduce the heat to low and simmer for about 7-15 minutes or until the veggies are tender, taking care not to overcook.
5. Stir in the basil and cook for another 1 minute. Remove the bay leaf and serve.

Zucchini Crispy Chips with Tofu Cheese

Prep Time: 10 minutes / Cook Time: 15 minutes

Serves: 2

Preferred spiralizer: Hourglass

Gluten-free

Good points: This recipe is very high in vitamin C; it is low in sodium and has no cholesterol

Nutritional Information Per Serving: Calories: 241;

Total Fat: 23.1g; Saturated Fat: 3.4g; Trans Fat: 0g;

Cholesterol: 0mg; Sodium: 25mg; Potassium: 577mg;

Total Carbs: 7.3g; Dietary Fiber: 2.5g; Sugar: 3.7g;

Protein: 5.9g; Vitamin A 8%; Calcium: 12%;

Vitamin C: 56%; Iron: 8%.

Ingredients:

- 2 zucchinis, spiralized
- 3 tablespoons of olive oil
- 3 oz. of tofu cheese, grated
- Salt and pepper to taste

Directions:

1. Preheat the oven to 350F.
2. Spiralize the zucchini into thin slices and coat them with olive oil.
3. Season the zucchini slices with salt and pepper.
4. Place the slices on a baking tray, previously lined with baking paper, and bake in the oven for 10-12 minutes.
5. Remove the zucchini slices from the oven, place them on the serving dish and sprinkle over the tofu cheese. Enjoy!

Summer Panzanella

Prep Time: 10 minutes / Cook Time: 0 minutes

Serves: 6

Preferred spiralizer: Hourglass

Vegetarian-friendly

Good points: This recipe is very high in vitamin B6, high in vitamin C, and has no cholesterol

Nutritional Information Per Serving: Calories: 146;

Total Fat: 9.1g; Saturated Fat: 1.4g; Trans Fat: 0g;

Cholesterol: 0mg; Sodium: 96mg; Potassium: 255mg;

Total Carbs: 14.8g; Dietary Fiber: 2g; Sugar: 2.4g;

Protein: 3.2g; Vitamin A: 12%; Calcium: 3%;

Vitamin C: 20%; Iron: 10%

Ingredients:

- 1 large-sized or 2 medium-sized heirloom tomatoes, cut into bite-size pieces
- 1 zucchini, medium-sized, spiralizer into noodles
- 1 ear corn, shucked

- 80 grams' stale baguette, torn into bite size pieces
- 1 tablespoon balsamic vinegar
- 1/2 cup basil leaves, chopped
- 1/4 cup chives, finely chopped
- 1/4 cup mint leaves, chopped
- 1/4 cup olive oil
- 2 tablespoons red wine vinegar

Directions:

1. In a large-sized bowl, whisk the red wine vinegar, olive oil, balsamic vinegar, a hearty pinch salt.
2. With a sharp knife, cut the corn kernels from the cob. Add the corn to the bowl.
3. Add the tomatoes, chopped herbs, torn baguette, and zoodles, and toss to combine.
4. Season with pepper and salt to taste. Serve.

Vegetable Noodles and Tofu

Prep Time: 10 minutes / Cook Time: 20 minutes

Serves: 8

Preferred spiralizer: Hourglass

Vegetarian-friendly

Good points: This recipe is very high in manganese, vitamin B6, and vitamin C, high in calcium, fiber, iron, magnesium, phosphorus, potassium, and selenium, and has no cholesterol

Nutritional Information Per Serving: Calories: 95;

Total Fat: 2.6g; Saturated Fat: 0.5g; Trans Fat: 0g;

Cholesterol: 0mg; Sodium: 485mg; Potassium: 421mg;

Total Carbs: 13.1g; Dietary Fiber: 2.7g; Sugar: 3.9g;

Protein: 6.7g; Vitamin A: 9%; Calcium: 14%;

Vitamin C: 36%; Iron: 16%

Ingredients:

- 1 zucchini, large-sized, spiralized
- 3 sweet potatoes, medium sized, peeled and then spiralized
- 16 ounces' tofu, drained and pressed
- 2 baby bok choy, stalks separated
- 1/4 cup tamari OR soy sauce
- 2 garlic cloves, minced
- 2 inches' fresh ginger, thinly sliced
- 4 scallions, chopped
- 8 cups water
- Toasted sesame seeds and sliced scallions, for serving

Directions:

1. In a large-sized pot, combine the ginger garlic, scallions, water, and soy sauce, and bring to a boil. When boiling, reduce to a simmer and cook for 10 minutes.
2. Meanwhile, add oil to grill pan and heat over medium-high heat. Spiralized the zucchini into zoodles. Sprinkle with pepper and salt.
3. Grill the tofu for 3 minutes each side or until grill marks appear. Set aside until ready to eat.
4. After the broth is simmered for 10 minutes, add the sweet potatoes and the zucchini. Cover and simmer for 10 minutes. Taste the broth and season with pepper and, if desired, with more soy sauce.
5. Serve the soup top with sesame seeds and scallions as garnish.

Spiralized Zucchini and Corn on the Cob Salad

Prep Time: 10 minutes / Cook Time: 7-8 minutes

Serves: 3

Preferred spiralizer: Hourglass

Vegetarian-friendly

Good points: This recipe is very high in vitamin B6, high in vitamin C, very low in sodium, and has no cholesterol

Nutritional Information Per Serving: Calories: 254;

Total Fat: 23.3g; Saturated Fat: 3.4g; Trans Fat: 0g;

Cholesterol: 0mg; Sodium: 18mg; Potassium: 394mg;

Total Carbs: 13.2g; Dietary Fiber: 2.5g; Sugar: 3.8g;

Protein: 2.8g; Vitamin A: 8%; Calcium: 1%;

Vitamin C: 38%; Iron: 9%

Ingredients:

- 1 corn cob, boiled
- 1 zucchini
- 1/2 cup cherry tomatoes
- 1/3 cup olive oil
- 2 tablespoons fresh squeezed lemon juice
- Salt and pepper

Directions:

1. Whisk the olive oil with the lemon juice, salt, and pepper and set aside.
2. Spiralize the zucchini into noodles.
3. Cut the cherry tomatoes into halves.
4. Boil the corn for about 7 to 8 minutes in unsalted water.
5. In a bowl, mix the zoodles, corn, and tomatoes. Drizzle with salad dressing.

The Ultimate Green Vegetable Bowl

Prep Time: 10 minutes / Cook Time: 7 minutes

Serves: 5

Preferred spiralizer: Hourglass

Vegetarian-friendly

Good points: This recipe is vitamin C, low in sodium, and has no cholesterol

Nutritional Information Per Serving: Calories: 280;

Total Fat: 24.1g; Saturated Fat: 3.4 g; Trans Fat: 0g;

Cholesterol: 0mg; Sodium: 145mg; Potassium: 539mg;

Total Carbs: 14.3g; Dietary Fiber: 4.9g; Sugar: 5g;

Protein: 6.3g; Vitamin A: 23%; Calcium: 6%;

Vitamin C: 135%; Iron: 10%

Ingredients:

- 3 cups broccoli, chopped (about 1 head)
- 2 medium zucchinis
- 1 1/2 cups snap peas
- 1/4 teaspoon salt, PLUS more to taste
- 1/4 cup nuts (recommend 1/8 cup cashews and 1/8 cup walnuts)
- 1/2 cup olive oil
- 1 ounce basil
- 1 clove garlic
- Hemp hearts, for topping, optional

Directions:

1. With a spiralizer, spiralize the zucchini into noodles and set aside.
2. Put the snap peas and broccoli into a microwavable steamer and microwave for 4 minutes. Put the zoodles on top and steam for 3 minutes or until the snap peas and broccoli are tender and the zucchini noodles are only slightly crunchy.
3. While the veggies are in the microwave, put the nuts, basil, garlic, olive oil, and salt in a blender and blend until smooth.
4. Pour the pesto into the steamer with the vegetables and mix. Divide between serving bowls. Season to taste with salt and then top with hemp hearts. Serve!

Vegan Parmesan Cauliflower Steaks Over Hemp Pesto Zoodles

Prep Time: 10 minutes / Cook Time: 40 minutes

Serves: 5

Preferred spiralizer: Hourglass

Vegetarian-friendly

Good points: This recipe is very high in vitamin B6 and vitamin C, high in iron, manganese, magnesium, and phosphorus, and has no cholesterol

Nutritional Information Per Serving: Calories: 251;

Total Fat: 18.9g; Saturated Fat: 2.7g; Trans Fat: 0g;

Cholesterol: 0mg; Sodium: 620mg; Potassium: 613mg;

Total Carbs: 14.7g; Dietary Fiber: 6.3g; Sugar: 3.3g;

Protein: 9g; Vitamin A: 4%; Calcium: 6%;

Vitamin C: 61%; Iron: 27%

Ingredients:

- 1 head cauliflower, medium-sized
- 2 1/2 zucchinis, medium-sized
- 1 teaspoon garlic, minced (about 2 cloves)
- 1/2 cup raw cashews
- 1/2 lemon, juiced
- 1/2 teaspoon salt
- 1/3 cup fresh basil leaves, packed
- 1/4 cup almond milk, unsweetened
- 1/4 cup PLUS 2 tablespoons hemp seeds, divided
- 1/4 cup walnuts or pine nuts
- 1/4 teaspoon garlic powder
- 1/4 teaspoon pepper
- 1/8 teaspoon black pepper
- 2 tablespoons nutritional yeast
- 2 tablespoons olive oil
- 3/4 teaspoon salt
- Cooking spray or olive oil

Directions:

1. Preheat the oven to 400F.
2. Lightly grease a baking sheet with nonstick spray or olive oil.
3. In a blender or a food processor, add the nutritional yeast, cashews, garlic powder, pepper, and salt, and process until resembling fine sand. Stir in 2 tablespoons hemp seeds.
4. Remove the leaves from the cauliflower. Vertically slice the cauliflower into 3/4-inch steaks, getting about 4-5 slices. Sprinkle both sides of the cauliflower steaks with the cashew parmesan cheese mix.
5. Bake for 40 to 45 minutes or until the edges of the cauliflower are slightly browned and crispy.
6. While the cauliflower is cooking, spiralizer the zucchinis into noodles. Put in a large-sized bowl.

7. In a blender or food processor, add the 1/4 cup of hemp seeds, almond milk, olive oil, walnuts, lemon juice, basil, garlic, pepper, and salt. Process or blend until smooth. Pour the sauce over the oodles and toss to combine.
8. Divide the zoodles between 5 plates and top each with a cauliflower steak.

Sweet Carrot Noodles with Broccoli and Tofu

Prep Time: 10 minutes / Cook Time: 15 minutes

Serves: 4

Preferred spiralizer: Hand-crank

Gluten-free

Good points: This recipe is high in calcium and manganese, and it is low in sodium

Nutritional Information Per Serving: Calories: 163;

Total Fat: 10.1g; Saturated Fat: 1.6g; Trans Fat: 0g;

Cholesterol: 0mg; Sodium: 47mg; Potassium: 461mg;

Total Carbs: 14g; Dietary Fiber: 3.7g; Sugar: 6.4g;

Protein: 7.5g; Vitamin A 127%; Calcium: 18%;

Vitamin C: 171%; Iron: 13%

Ingredients:

- 2 cups of broccoli, separated into small florets
- 1 cup of tofu
- 2 large carrots, spiralized
- 1 teaspoon. of sugar
- 1 small onion, diced
- 2 cloves of garlic, minced
- 1 small green bell pepper, diced
- 1 teaspoon of cumin
- 1 teaspoon of turmeric
- 2 tablespoons of olive oil
- Salt and pepper, to taste

Directions:

1. In a medium-sized pot, boil the broccoli for 2-3 minutes in salted water.
2. Heat the olive oil in a large pan. Add in the garlic, the onion and the pepper. Cook for 5 minutes.
3. Add in the tofu, the broccoli and season with the cumin and turmeric. Cook for another 5 minutes. Remove from the heat and place the mixture in the serving dishes.
4. Heat the remaining olive oil in a small skillet and add the carrot noodles. Cook for 2 minutes, then add the sugar and cook for 2 minutes more, or until the sugar has melted.
5. Add the caramelized carrot noodles to the serving dishes. Enjoy!

Zucchini Pasta with Chicken

Prep Time: 10 minutes / Cook Time: 20 minutes

Serves: 2

Preferred spiralizer: Hourglass

Gluten-free, Paleo-friendly

Good points: This recipe is high in vitamins B6, B12 and C, and it is low in saturated fat

Nutritional Information Per Serving: Calories: 547;

Total Fat: 22.6; Saturated Fat: 2.1g; Trans Fat: 0g;

Cholesterol: 194mg; Sodium: 282mg; Potassium: 1186mg;

Total Carbs: 11.6g; Dietary Fiber: 3.2g; Sugar: 5.5g;

Protein: 76g; Vitamin A 20%; Calcium: 9%;

Vitamin C: 64%; Iron: 22%.

Ingredients:

- 1 pound of chicken breast, boneless and diced
- 2 cloves of garlic
- 1 large zucchini, spiralized into large noodles
- ½ cup of cherry tomatoes, diced
- 1 small onion, diced
- 1/2 cup of basil
- 2 tablespoons of extra virgin olive oil
- Salt and pepper, to taste

Directions:

1. Place a large pan over medium heat. Heat the olive oil, add the chicken and season it with salt and pepper. Cook for 3 minutes.
2. Add the garlic, the onion and the cherry tomatoes. Mix well and cook until the mixture is reduced.
3. Add the basil, mix it in and add more salt or pepper if needed.
4. Mix in the zucchini noodles and toss well. Cook for another 2 minutes.
5. Remove from the heat and serve.

Sausage, Broccoli Rabe and Parsnip Pasta

Prep Time: 7 minutes / Cook Time: 13 minutes

Serves: 2-4

Preferred spiralizer: Hourglass

Vegetarian-friendly

Good points: This recipe is very high in vitamin C, high in calcium, fiber, manganese, phosphorus, and vitamin A

Nutritional Information Per Serving: Calories: 107;

Total Fat: 4.4 g; Saturated Fat: 2.1g; Trans Fat: 0g;

Cholesterol: 13mg; Sodium: 245mg; Potassium: 269mg;

Total Carbs: 11.7g; Dietary Fiber: 2.9g; Sugar: 2.8g;

Protein: 6.1g; Vitamin A: 11%; Calcium: 13%;

Vitamin C: 27%; Iron: 4%

Ingredients:

- 1 bunch broccoli rabe, stems trimmed
- 2 parsnips, peeled and then spiralized, noodles cut into shorter strands
- 2 links spicy chicken Italian Sausage, casings removed
- 2 cloves garlic, minced
- 1/4 teaspoon crushed red pepper flakes
- 1/2 teaspoon dried oregano
- 1/2 cup parmesan cheese, grated
- 1/2 cup chicken broth, low sodium
- kosher salt and black pepper

Directions:

1. Chop the broccoli rabe into 1-inch pieces and set aside.
2. Put a large-sized skillet on medium heat. When the skillet is hot, add the sausage and oregano. Cook for about 6 to 8 minutes or until browned, breaking the pieces in the process. Transfer to a plate.
3. Add the broccoli rabe and the parsnip noodles into the skillet. Add the red pepper, garlic, and broth. Cook for about 5 minutes or until al dente.

4. Return the sausage into the skillet. Add the cheese and then stir to combine.

Butternut Squash Pasta

Prep Time: 10 minutes / Cook Time: 15 minutes

Serves: 2

Preferred spiralizer: Hourglass

Vegetarian-friendly

Good points: This recipe is very high in vitamin A and vitamin C, and high in phosphorus and calcium

Nutritional Information Per Serving: Calories: 223;

Total Fat: 16.2g; Saturated Fat: 10.4g; Trans Fat: 0g;

Cholesterol: 46mg; Sodium: 286mg; Potassium: 424mg;

Total Carbs: 14.3g; Dietary Fiber: 2.4g; Sugar: 2.5g;

Protein: 8.2g; Vitamin A: 258%; Calcium: 25%;

Vitamin C: 48 %; Iron: 6%

Ingredients:

- 1/2-pound butternut squash
- 2 tablespoons butter, divided
- 2 tablespoons fresh parsley OR another herb, divided
- 3 tablespoons parmesan cheese, divided
- Olive oil
- Salt and pepper, to taste

Directions:

1. Preheat the oven to 400F.
2. Cut the ends from the squash, cut into halves, and peel the half that you plan to use.
3. Put the squash in a spiralizer and spiralizer into noodles.
4. Put the squash noodles into a baking sheet. Drizzle with the olive oil and sprinkle with salt and pepper. Toss to coat well. Bake for about 10-12 minutes or until the pasta is tender, but not crispy.

5. Plate between 2 plates. Top each with half the butter, half the cheese, and half the parsley.

Carrot Pasta with Ginger-Lime Peanut Sauce

Prep Time: 15 minutes / Cook Time: 0 minutes

Serves: 4-6

Preferred spiralizer: Hourglass

Vegetarian-friendly

Good points: This recipe is very high in vitamin A and vitamin B6, high in manganese, and has no cholesterol

Nutritional Information Per Serving: Calories: 158;

Total Fat: 10.4g; Saturated Fat: 4.1g; Trans Fat: 0g;

Cholesterol: 0mg; Sodium: 516mg; Potassium: 396mg;

Total Carbs: 13.8; Dietary Fiber: 2.9g; Sugar: 5.2g;

Protein: 4.8g; Vitamin A: 242%; Calcium: 4%;

Vitamin C: 10 %; Iron: 10%

Ingredients:

For the carrot pasta:

- 5 carrots, large-sized, peeled and then spiraled into noodles
- 2 tablespoons fresh cilantro, finely chopped
- 1/3 cup roasted cashews

For the Ginger-Lime Peanut Sauce:

- 1 tablespoon fresh ginger, peeled and grated
- 1 tablespoon lime juice
- 2 large cloves garlic, finely chopped
- 2 tablespoons creamy peanut butter
- 2 tablespoons liquid aminos
- 4 tablespoons coconut milk

- Kosher salt, to taste
- Pinch cayenne pepper

Directions:

1. In a small-sized bowl, combine all the ingredients until creamy and smooth.
2. Wash the carrots, peel, and then pat dry.
3. Spiralizer the carrots into noodles and grate the rest of the carrots that can no longer be spiralized.
4. Put all the carrot noodles into a large-sized servings bowl.
5. Pour the sauce over the noodles and toss.
6. Serve with roasted cashews and fresh chopped cilantro.

Rustic Chorizo Pasta

Prep Time: 10 minutes / Cook Time: 20 minutes

Serves:

Preferred spiralizer: Hourglass

Vegetarian-friendly

Good points: This recipe is low in sugar

Nutritional Information Per Serving: Calories: 556;

Total Fat: 43.8g; Saturated Fat: 16.4g; Trans Fat: 0g;

Cholesterol: 100mg; Sodium: 1650mg; Potassium: 975mg;

Total Carbs: 10.8g; Dietary Fiber: 2.7g; Sugar: 5g;

Protein: 29.6g; Vitamin A: 21%; Calcium: 4%;

Vitamin C: 53%; Iron: 14%

Ingredients:

- 1 pound chorizo
- 14.5 oz. canned diced tomatoes
- 2 zucchinis, peeled and then spiralized
- 1/2 sweet onion, diced
- 1/2 teaspoon pepper

- 1/2 teaspoon sea salt
- Fresh parsley, for garnish, optional

Directions:

1. In a large-sized skillet, break the chorizo apart and brown.
2. Transfer to a bowl, reserving the juices that the chorizo releases.
3. Add the onion in the skillet and cook until soft.
4. Return the chorizo into the skillet. Add the diced tomato and sprinkle with the salt and pepper. Simmer for 10 minutes.
5. You can serve this sauce on top of raw zoodles. Or, you can add the zoodles and cook for about 5 minutes.
6. Sprinkle with parsley and serve.

Taco Chicken Zucchini Pasta

Prep Time: 10 minutes / Cook Time: 20 minutes

Serves:

Preferred spiralizer: Hourglass

Vegetarian-friendly

Good points: This recipe is high in niacin, selenium, and vitamin B6, and low in sodium and sugar

Nutritional Information Per Serving: Calories: 511;

Total Fat: 29g; Saturated Fat: 7.7g; Trans Fat: 0g;

Cholesterol: 151mg; Sodium: 167mg; Potassium: 975mg;

Total Carbs: 11.1g; Dietary Fiber: 6.2g; Sugar: 2.2g;

Protein: 51.9 g; Vitamin A: 10%; Calcium: 6%;

Vitamin C: 34%; Iron: 20%

Ingredients:

- 1 1/2 pounds' chicken breasts, boneless, skinless, cut into small chunks
- 1 zucchini, spiralized – as much as you like (I used 3 small/medium zucchinis)
- 1 teaspoon chili powder

- 1 teaspoon coconut oil for nonstick pan OR 1 tablespoon coconut oil for regular pan
- 1 teaspoon garlic powder
- 1 teaspoon ground cumin
- 1 teaspoon onion powder

For the sauce:

- 1 1/2 medium avocados
- 1 teaspoon garlic powder
- 1 teaspoon ground cumin
- 1 teaspoon onion powder
- 2 tablespoons lemon juice
- Water, as needed to get a good consistency

Directions:

1. Spiralize the zucchini into noodles and put into a large-sized bowl.
2. Put the coconut oil in a skillet and add the chicken. Add the spices and cook, frequently stirring, until the chicken is done. The smaller you cut your chicken, the faster the meat will cook.
3. In a blender, put all the sauce ingredients together and blend until very smooth. Add water as need to thin it into thick sauce-like consistency – do not overdo the water.
4. Stir the sauce into the zoodles. Add the chicken. Season to taste with salt and pepper. Serve.

Cajun Zucchini Noodle Pasta (Vegan, Paleo)

Prep Time: 35 minutes / Cook Time: 15-16 minutes

Serves: 2

Preferred spiralizer: Hourglass

Vegetarian, paleo and vegan-friendly

Good points: This recipe is very high in potassium, riboflavin, vitamin A, vitamin B6, and vitamin C, high in fiber, iron, niacin, pantothenic acid, and phosphorus, and has no cholesterol

Nutritional Information Per Serving: Calories: 93;

Total Fat: 4g; Saturated Fat: 3g; Trans Fat: 0g;

Cholesterol: 0mg; Sodium: 82mg; Potassium: 715mg;

Total Carbs: 13.3g; Dietary Fiber: 3.5g; Sugar: 7.9g;

Protein: 4.3g; Vitamin A: 54%; Calcium: 3%;

Vitamin C: 23%; Iron: 14%

Ingredients:

- 8 ounces' mushrooms, sliced
- 2 zucchini squash, peeled (about 1 pounds)
- 2 tomatoes, chopped
- 2 teaspoons Cajun seasoning
- 1/2 red onion, thinly sliced
- 1 tablespoon coconut oil
- 1 red bell pepper, thinly sliced
- 1 green bell pepper, thinly sliced
- Salt and pepper, to taste

Directions:

1. Spiralize the zucchini into noodles. Put the noodles into a large-sized mesh strainer and generously sprinkle with salt. Toss well and let sit over the bowl to catch the moisture they release. Set aside for 30 minutes.
2. Put the coconut oil in a deep skillet or a Dutch oven and melt over medium heat. Add the peppers and onions and sauté for about 8 minutes. Add the mushrooms and tomatoes. If desired, add your desired meat at this point. Sauté for 5 more minutes.
3. When the zoodles are sweated, rinse well with water and then pat dry using a towel. Add into the skillet. Add the Cajun seasoning and stir well – start with a smallest amount if you don't like spicy food. Cook for about 2 -3 minutes and then season with salt and pepper to taste. Serve warm.

Sausage Zoodle Pizza Bake

Prep Time: 20 minutes / Cook Time: 25 minutes

Serves: 6

Preferred spiralizer: Hourglass

Vegetarian-friendly

Good points: This recipe is very high vitamin B6, vitamin B12, and vitamin C, and high in riboflavin and phosphorus

Nutritional Information Per Serving: Calories: 171;

Total Fat: 8.6g; Saturated Fat: 3.2g; Trans Fat: 0g;

Cholesterol: 73mg; Sodium: 728mg; Potassium: 454mg;

Total Carbs: 14.4g; Dietary Fiber: 2.5g; Sugar: 3.7g;

Protein: 10.7g; Vitamin A: 15%; Calcium: 8%;

Vitamin C: 73%; Iron: 11%

Ingredients:

- 3-4 zucchini, large-sized (about 2 pounds)
- 3 ounces' mild Italian sausage (about 1 piece 5-inch link, casing removed)
- 2 eggs, lightly beaten
- 1/2 cup mushrooms, sliced (cremini or white)
- 1 1/2 cups mozzarella cheese, shredded, divided
- 2 tablespoons cornmeal
- 1/4 cup Parmesan cheese, grated
- 1/4 cup black olives, sliced
- 1/4 cup all-purpose flour
- 1/2 cup pizza sauce (4 ounces) OR marinara sauce
- 1/2 bell pepper, cut into stripes (or any color bell pepper)
- 1 teaspoon salt
- Basil, fresh chopped, for garnish, optional

Directions:

1. Preheat the oven to 400F. Coat a 9-inch pie pan or a 2-quart baking dish with cooking spray. Spiralizer the zucchini into noodles and put the zoodles in a colander. Sprinkle with salt and toss to incorporate. Let stand for 15 to 20 minutes in a colander to remove excess water.
2. Meanwhile, cook the sausage in a large-sized frying pan. Set aside.
3. When the zucchini has rested for 15 minutes and with tea towel or paper towels, dry gently to release any excess water. Set aside.
4. In a large-sized bowl, combine the eggs with parmesan cheese, 1/2 cup mozzarella cheese, cornmeal, and flour.
5. Add the zoodles and stir to incorporate. Transfer into the prepared pie pan. Bake for about 15 minutes or until set and no excess liquid remains.

6. Remove from the oven and then spread with the pizza sauce. Top with the remaining mozzarella cheese, mushrooms, sausage, bell pepper, and olive. Bake for 15 minutes more or until the cheese is bubbly, melted, and light brown. Remove from the oven and let rest for 2 to 3 minutes. Serve. If desired, garnish with freshly chopped basil.

Margherita Spiralized Pizza

Prep Time: 30 minutes / Cook Time: 25 minutes

Serves: 6

Preferred spiralizer: Hourglass

Vegetarian-friendly and gluten-free

Good points: This recipe is very high in vitamin B6 and B12, and high in phosphorus and vitamin C

Nutritional Information Per Serving: Calories: 191;

Total Fat: 10.4g; Saturated Fat: 3.6g; Trans Fat: 0g;

Cholesterol: 67mg; Sodium: 408mg; Potassium: 461mg;

Total Carbs: 15.3g; Dietary Fiber: 2.5g; Sugar: 3g;

Protein: 10.5g; Vitamin A: 5%; Calcium: 29%;

Vitamin C: 4%; Iron: 6%

Ingredients:

- 1 cup tomato basil sauce
- 2 eggs
- 2 potatoes, peeled, and spiralized using the Blade C (Idaho or sweet potato)
- 2 tablespoon olive oil, divided
- 3 teaspoon garlic powder, divided 2 teaspoons and 1 teaspoon
- 5 leaves basil
- 5 quarter-inch slices mozzarella cheese
- Parmesan cheese, to top
- Salt and pepper, to taste

Directions:

1. Put a large-sized skillet on medium heat. Pour 1 tablespoon of olive oil in the skillet. When the oil is hot, add the potato noodles and season with pepper, salt, and first 2 teaspoon garlic powder. Cook the noodles, stirring every 30 seconds to 1 minute or until the potato noodles smell cooked and soften. If using sweet potato, the noodles will turn a deeper orange. If using an Idaho potatoes, the noodles will turn slightly brown and become sticky.
2. When the noodles are cooked, put in a large-sized bowl and crack in the eggs. Mix well until combined.
3. Pour the noodles into a 10-inch skillet. Make sure the noodles, evenly spreading so you can't see the bottom of the skillet.
4. When the noodles are set, lay a baking paper or a plastic wrap over the noodles.
5. Put a pot over the plastic wrap or paper and press down slowly and firmly – condense and flatten as much as possible. Put something heavy inside the pot to add additional weight. Put in the fridge and let sit for 15 to 20 minutes – the longer the better.
6. Take the skillet out and put over medium heat. Put a large 10 to 12-inch skillet, but do not turn the heat on. Do not move the skillet with the potato noodles for 5 minutes and let cook.
7. Turn the heat on to medium underneath the skillet without the noodles and pour 1 tablespoon of olive oil in the skillet. When the oil is hot, flip the noodle skillet over and into the new skillet. If any noodle go out of place, simple hold them using a spatula or wooden spoon. Fry for 5 to 7 minutes. While the crust is cooking, set the oven to broil.
8. When both sides are crispy and the noodles have become the crust, turn the heat off.
9. Spread the tomato-basil sauce over the top of the pizza, leaving 1-2 inches of noodle crust between the edge and the sauce so you can hold them when eating.
10. Top with the mozzarella slices, pepper, salt, and 1 teaspoon of garlic powder. Put in the oven and broil for 7 to 10 minutes or until the mozzarella melts without browning and the crust becomes crispy.
11. Take out the oven, sprinkle with Parmesan cheese and then top with basil.

Carrot Noodles with Spinach and Pesto Pizza

Prep Time: 15 minutes / Cook Time: 15 minutes

Serves: 4

Preferred spiralizer: Hourglass

Vegetarian-free

Good points: This recipe is high in vitamins A and B6, and in calcium

Nutritional Information Per Serving: Calories: 168;

Total Fat: 21.1; Saturated Fat: 8.8g; Trans Fat: 0g;

Cholesterol: 37mg; Sodium: 475mg; Potassium: 301mg;

Total Carbs: 15.6g; Dietary Fiber: 2.2g; Sugar: 5.2g;

Protein: 13g; Vitamin A 206%; Calcium: 28%;

Vitamin C: 10%; Iron: 9%

Ingredients:

- 1 pre-baked pizza crust
- 1 cup of baby spinach
- 2 cups of carrots, spiralized
- 1 cup of mushrooms, sliced
- 1 cup of mozzarella cheese, sliced
- 1 cup of cheddar cheese, grated
- 1 tablespoon of vegetable oil
- ¼ cup of pesto sauce

Directions:

1. Preheat the oven to 400F. Brush the pizza crust with the vegetable oil before adding the pesto sauce.
2. Spread in equal measures the mushrooms, the spinach and the carrots.
3. Place the mozzarella slices on top and sprinkle over the cheddar cheese.
4. Place into the oven and cook for 12-15 minutes.
5. Remove from the heat, cut the pizza into slices and serve.

Sausage, Brussels Sprouts, and Spiralized Parsnip Pasta

Prep Time: 20 minutes / Cook Time: 20 minutes

Serves: 4

Preferred spiralizer: Hourglass

Vegetarian-friendly

Good points: This recipe is very high in vitamin C, high in fiber, manganese, and phosphorus

Nutritional Information Per Serving: Calories: 123;

Total Fat: 5.7g; Saturated Fat: 1.7g; Trans Fat: 0g;

Cholesterol: 9mg; Sodium: 353mg; Potassium: 397mg;

Total Carbs: 14.1g; Dietary Fiber: 3.7g; Sugar: 3.1g;

Protein: 5.6 g; Vitamin A: 9%; Calcium: 8%;

Vitamin C: 65%; Iron: 6%

Ingredients:

- 6 1/2 ounces (1 large-sized) parsnip, peeled, spiralized, and then trimmed 6-inches long
- 5 ounces Brussels sprouts, shredded
- 2 links spicy Chicken Italian Sausage, casings removed
- 2 teaspoons olive oil
- 2 cloves garlic, minced
- 1/4 teaspoon kosher salt
- 1/4 teaspoon crushed red pepper flakes
- 1/4 cup shallots, chopped
- 1/4 cup parmesan cheese, grated
- 1/2 cup chicken broth, low sodium
- Black pepper, to taste

Directions:

1. Put a large-sized, nonstick skillet on medium heat. When hot, add the sausage and cook for about 6-8 minutes until browned, breaking up the sausage in the process. Transfer into a plate.
2. Put the oil in the skillet. Add the garlic, shallots, and brussels sprouts. Cook over medium-high for about 4 to 5 minutes or until the edges are golden. Set aside with the sausage.
3. Add the parsnip noodles, bell pepper, red pepper flakes and broth into the skillet and reduce the heat over medium heat. Cook for about 5 minutes or until the noodles are al dente.
4. Return the sausage and Brussel sprouts into the skillet. Add the cheese and stir to mix.

Chicken Zucchini Pesto Noodles

Prep Time: minutes / Cook Time: minutes

Serves:

Preferred spiralizer: Hourglass

Vegetarian-friendly

Good points: This recipe is high in niacin, selenium, and vitamin B6, and low in sugar

Nutritional Information Per Serving: Calories: 325;

Total Fat: 17.2g; Saturated Fat: 7.1g; Trans Fat: 0g;

Cholesterol: 101mg; Sodium: 346mg; Potassium: 635mg;

Total Carbs: 7.4g; Dietary Fiber: 2.4g; Sugar: 2.9g;

Protein: 35.4g; Vitamin A: 7%; Calcium: 4%;

Vitamin C: 31%; Iron: 14%

Ingredients:

- 2 zucchinis, large-sized, spiralized
- 1 1/2 tablespoon chickpea flour
- 1 pound chicken breast, boneless, skinless
- 1 tablespoon olive oil
- 1 teaspoon fresh squeezed lemon juice
- 1/2 teaspoon sea salt
- 1/3 cup almond milk, plus more as needed
- 1/3 cup basil pesto
- 1/4 teaspoon ground black pepper

Directions:

1. In a large-sized skillet, put the olive oil and heat over medium-high heat.
2. Season the chicken with pepper and salt. Cook for 10 to 12 minutes or until the chicken is cooked through. Remove from the heat, slice, and set aside.
3. In the same skillet, whisk in the almond milk, pesto, and chickpea flour. Bring to a simmer.
4. Add the zoodles and continue cooking for another 4 to 5 minutes or until the oodles are mostly tender, yet slightly crisp.

5. Add the chicken, toss to coat. Add the fresh lemon juice and season with pepper and salt, as needed. Serve immediately.

DESSERTS

Chocolate Muffins with Zucchini Noodles and Cashews

Prep Time: 20 minutes / Cook Time: 40 minutes

Serves: 12

Preferred spiralizer: Hourglass

Good points: This recipe is high in iron and it has low cholesterol

Nutritional Information Per Serving: Calories: 132;

Total Fat: 8.8; Saturated Fat: 4.9g; Trans Fat: 0g;

Cholesterol: 43mg; Sodium: 174mg; Potassium: 147mg;

Total Carbs: 11g; Dietary Fiber: 1.1g; Sugar: 7.6g;

Protein: 3.2g; Vitamin A 2%; Calcium: 3%;

Vitamin C: 5%; Iron: 8%.

Ingredients:

- 1 zucchini, spiralized
- ½ cup of chocolate chips
- ½ cup of coconut flour
- ½ teaspoon of baking soda
- ½ teaspoon of salt
- ½ tablespoon of cinnamon
- 1 teaspoon of nutmeg
- 3 eggs
- 3 tablespoons of maple syrup
- 1 teaspoon of vanilla extract
- 1 tablespoon of coconut oil
- 2 tablespoons of almond milk
- ½ cup of cashews

Directions:

1. Preheat the oven to 300F.
2. Spray a muffin tin with olive oil and cover the portions with parchment paper.
3. Keep the zucchini noodles between paper towels, to remove the moisture.
4. Mix the coconut flour with the cinnamon, the nutmeg, the salt and the baking soda into a large bowl.
5. In another bowl, combine the eggs, the vanilla extract, the almond milk, the maple syrup, and the coconut oil. Whisk and mix well.
6. Add the content of the first bowl to the ones in the second bowl and mix well.
7. Add in the zucchini, the cashews and the chocolate chips and stir everything into a batter.
8. Pour this batter into the muffin tins and bake for 30-40 minutes.

9. Remove the tray from the oven and gently take the muffins out. Serve warm.

Spiralized Cinnamon Apple, Pecan, and Oats with Greek Yogurt

Prep Time: 20 minutes / Cook Time: 15-20 minutes

Serves: 4

Preferred spiralizer: Hourglass

Vegetarian-friendly

Good points: This recipe is very high in vitamin B6, and low in sodium and cholesterol

Nutritional Information Per Serving: Calories: 112;

Total Fat: 4.8g; Saturated Fat: 1.8g; Trans Fat: 0g;

Cholesterol: 5mg; Sodium: 26mg; Potassium: 165mg;

Total Carbs: 12.1g; Dietary Fiber: 2.2g; Sugar: 8.3g;

Protein: 6.5g; Vitamin A: 1%; Calcium: 6%;

Vitamin C: 8 %; Iron: 2%

Ingredients:

- 1 apple, medium-sized
- 1 tablespoon pecans, chopped
- 1 teaspoon brown sugar, divided
- 1 teaspoon lemon juice, fresh squeezed
- 1 teaspoon unsalted butter
- 1/2 teaspoon ground cinnamon
- 2 teaspoons old-fashioned oats
- 8 ounces' Greek yogurt, non-fat

Directions:

1. Using the smallest blade, spiralize the apple, leaving the peel on. Discard the seeds and core. Toss the apple zoodles with the lemon juice.
2. Heat the skillet medium heat. Toast the oats and pecans until fragrant and slightly golden.

3. Put the butter in skillet and melt. Add 1/4 teaspoon of brown sugar and cinnamon and cook until slightly caramelized. Remove from the heat.
4. Stir the remaining cinnamon into the Greek yogurt. Divide the yogurt between 4 bowls and top equally with the spiralized apple and pecan mix.

Spiralized Apple Pie Topping with Walnuts

Prep Time: 2 minutes / Cook Time: 5 minutes

Serves: 4

Preferred spiralizer: Hourglass

Vegetarian-friendly

Good points: This recipe is very high vitamin B6 and low in sodium

Nutritional Information Per Serving: Calories: 158;

Total Fat: 12.1g; Saturated Fat: 6g; Trans Fat: 0g;

Cholesterol: 24mg; Sodium: 66mg; Potassium: 124mg;

Total Carbs: 13.7g; Dietary Fiber: 3g; Sugar: 9.3g;

Protein: 1.5g; Vitamin A: 6%; Calcium: 1%;

Vitamin C: 11%; Iron: 3%

Ingredients:

- 2 firm apples, large-sized, spiralized
- 1 1/2 tablespoons brown sugar, low carb, recipe below
- 1/2 teaspoon ground cinnamon
- 1/8 teaspoon pure vanilla extract
- 3 tablespoons walnut halves, chopped
- 4 tablespoons pastured butter, divided
- Pinch sea salt, finely ground

Low Carb Brown Sugar (makes 1/4 cup brown sugar):

- 1/4 tablespoon molasses
- 1/4 cup sweetener

Directions:

1. Mix the molasses and the sweetener and store in airtight containers.
2. Wash the apples and remove the stems. Spiralizer the apples into noodles. Discard the seeds and the core, they will be easy to pick out.
3. Heat a frying pan over medium heat. When hot, add 2 tablespoons of butter, low carb sugar, salt, and cinnamon. Stir to combine and then add the walnuts.
4. Sauté for 1-2 minutes, constantly stirring. Add the apples and remaining 2 tablespoons butter.
5. Sauté for 2 minutes, constantly stirring, until soft. Remove from the heat and add the vanilla. Stir well and serve.

Honeydew and Cantaloupe Melon Salad

Prep Time: 20 minutes / Cook Time: 0 minutes

Serves: 10

Preferred spiralizer: Handheld Spiralizer

Vegetarian-friendly

Good points: This recipe is low in cholesterol, high in potassium and vitamin A, and very high in vitamin C

Nutritional Information Per Serving: Calories: 72;

Total Fat: 1.4g; Saturated Fat: 0.8g; Trans Fat: 0g;

Cholesterol: 5mg; Sodium: 42mg; Potassium: 376mg;

Total Carbs: 15.3g; Dietary Fiber: 1.6g; Sugar: 13.1g;

Protein: 1.9g; Vitamin A: 11%; Calcium: 5%;

Vitamin C: 47%; Iron: 2%

Ingredients:

- 1 honeydew melon
- 1 cantaloupe
- 1o tablespoons evaporated milk sweetened with 10 teaspoons low carb sweetener or 5 packets stevia sweetener

Directions:

1. Cut the honeydew melon into halves and then scoop the seeds out. Cut into 2-inch wide sections and, using a paring knife, remove the skin and cut into 2-inch squares.
2. Put each melon square on the top of a hand-held spiralizer. Press down firmly on the top of the melon using the spiralizer hand guard. Turn the handle clockwise until all the melon squares are spiralized. Remove any excess scraps.
3. Repeat the process with the cantaloupe.
4. When ready to serve, mix the evaporated milk with the low carb sweetener. Drizzle with the low carb milk.

Jarred Apple Pie

Prep Time: 5 minutes / Cook Time: 0 minutes

Serves: 5

Preferred spiralizer: Hourglass

Vegetarian-friendly

Good points: This recipe has no cholesterol, very low in sodium, high in fiber, manganese, and vitamin C, and very high in vitamin B6

Nutritional Information Per Serving: Calories: 105;

Total Fat: 5.3g; Saturated Fat: 1.5g; Trans Fat: 0g;

Cholesterol: 0mg; Sodium: 2mg; Potassium: 162mg;

Total Carbs: 14.8g; Dietary Fiber: 2.9g; Sugar: 10.7g;

Protein: 2g; Vitamin A: 5%; Calcium: 1%;

Vitamin C: 14%; Iron: 4%

Ingredients:

- 2 red apples
- 1/4 cup walnuts, finely chopped
- 1/4 cup sultanas
- 1/2 teaspoon ground cinnamon
- 2 teaspoon lemon juice

Optional:

- About 2 tablespoons coconut cream

Directions:

1. Spiralize the apples using the fine spiralizer attachment to make thin apple noodles.
2. Put the apple noodles into a bowl. Add the rest of the ingredients. Toss to coat the apples noodles with lemon juice –this will prevent them from browning.
3. Transfer to serving jars or bowls. Top each serving with coconut cream. Sprinkle with additional chopped walnuts.

Sweet Potato Bars

Prep Time: 10 minutes / Cook Time: 35 minutes

Serves: 16

Preferred spiralizer: Hourglass

Vegetarian-friendly

Good points: This recipe is very low in cholesterol and sodium, high in manganese, and very high in vitamin B6

Nutritional Information Per Serving: Calories: 189;

Total Fat: 15.8g; Saturated Fat: 7g; Trans Fat: 0g;

Cholesterol: 4mg; Sodium: 25mg; Potassium: 258mg;

Total Carbs: 14.1g; Dietary Fiber: 3.8g; Sugar: 5.9g;

Protein: 2.4g; Vitamin A: 3%; Calcium: 2%;

Vitamin C: 17%; Iron: 10%

Ingredients:

For the sweet potatoes:

- 4 sweet potatoes, medium-sized, peeled and then spiralized
- 2 tablespoons organic butter melted OR coconut oil

- 1/2 teaspoon cinnamon
- 1 tablespoon pure maple syrup
- 1 tablespoon organic coconut sugar OR raw cane sugar

For the pecan topping:

- 2 tablespoons pure maple syrup
- 1 1/2 cups raw pecans, whole or chopped

For the sweet coconut sauce:

- 3/4 cup powdered sugar (18 packets stevia or 2 tsp liquid stevia)
- 1 can coconut cream

Directions:

For the sweet potatoes:

1. Spiralize the sweet potatoes into noodles and put into a mixing bowl. Add the cinnamon, coconut sugar, maple, syrup, and butter. Stir gently to combine.
2. Transfer into a baking dish and bake in a preheated 375F oven for about 10 to 15 minutes or until the sweet potato noodles are soft.
3. When the potato noodles are soft, turn the oven to a broil at 400F and broil for 10 minutes or until slightly crisp.

For the pecan topping:

1. Put the pecans into a frying pan. Roast for about 5 minutes, occasionally stirring. Add the maple syrup and cook for 5 minutes more, occasionally stirring, until the maples syrup crystalizes around the pecans – they should become grainy in texture.
2. Immediately transfer into a bowl and set aside.

For the sweet coconut sauce:

1. Scoop the coconut cream into kitchen aid or a mixing bowl; beat until whipped consistency.
2. Add the sweetener and whip again.
3. Add 2 tablespoon of the coconut liquid from the coconut cream can.
4. Whip again until the consistency is like thick salad dressing.

To assemble:

1. Pour 1/2 of the coconut sauce over the bakes sweet potato noodles – do not pour all the sauce – leave some in a pouring cup to serve on the side to add for each serving.
2. Sprinkle with the pecan topping. Serve hot.

Two-Ingredient Cinnamon Apple Spiral Pancakes

Prep Time: 5 minutes / Cook Time: 10 minutes

Serves: 12

Preferred spiralizer: Hourglass

Vegetarian-friendly

Good points: This recipe is low in sodium, high in manganese and selenium, ad very high in vitamin B6.

Nutritional Information Per Serving: Calories: 72;

Total Fat: 2.3g; Saturated Fat: 1.1g; Trans Fat: 0g;

Cholesterol: 55mg; Sodium: 22mg; Potassium: 124mg;

Total Carbs: 11.7g; Dietary Fiber: 1g; Sugar: 8.4g;

Protein: 2.1g; Vitamin A: 2%; Calcium: 1%;

Vitamin C: 5%; Iron: 3%

Ingredients:

- 1 apple, spiralized using the Blade D
- 2 ripe bananas, medium-sized
- 1/4 teaspoon cinnamon
- 2 teaspoons coconut oil
- 4 eggs, large-sized, beaten
- Maple syrup, to serve

Directions:

1. Put the bananas into a bowl. Mash using a fork until no large clumps remain. If you have enough time, mix using an electric mixer to blend until no clumps remain. Add the eggs in and then mix thoroughly until combined.
2. Heat a large-sized skillet or a griddle over medium-high heat. When the skillet/griddle is hot, coat with nonstick cooking spray. Ladle 2 tablespoons of pancake mixture at a time and cook the pancakes for about 1 to 2 minutes or until the bottom is set.
3. Flip and cook for 2 minutes more or until the pancakes are cooked through and slightly browned – these pancakes will not be fluffy; they will be flat. Repeat process until all the batter is cooked, transferring the cooked pancakes into a plate when they are cooked.
4. When all the pancakes are cooked, put the coconut oil in the skillet and swirl to coat. Add the apple noodles, sprinkle with cinnamon, and cook for about 2 to 3 minutes or until wilted.
5. Serve pancakes topped with the cinnamon apple noodles, drizzle with maple syrup, and serve.

Cinnamon Sweet Potato Apple Waffles

Prep Time: 15 minutes / Cook Time: 10 minutes

Serves: 4

Preferred spiralizer: Hourglass

Vegetarian-friendly

Good points: This recipe is low in sodium, high in fiber, iron, and manganese, and very high in vitamin B6 and vitamin C.

Nutritional Information Per Serving: Calories: 73;

Total Fat: 1.4g; Saturated Fat: 0g; Trans Fat: 0g;

Cholesterol: 41mg; Sodium: 26mg; Potassium: 212mg;

Total Carbs: 14.2g; Dietary Fiber: 2.6g; Sugar: 7.7g;

Protein: 2.1g; Vitamin A: 3%; Calcium: 1%;

Vitamin C: 23%; Iron: 8%

Ingredients:

- 1 apple

- 1 egg, lightly beaten
- 1 sweet potato, large-sized, spiralized
- 1 teaspoon cinnamon
- Cooking spray

Directions:

1. Preheat a waffle iron.
2. Grease a medium skillet with nonstick cooking spray and heat on medium-high heat. Add the sweet potato noodles and cook for about 8-10 minutes, frequently stirring, until tender and soft.
3. While the sweet potato noodles are cooking, grate the apples with a grater using the large holes. Alternatively, you can also spiralizer the apple – just be sure to remove the seeds. Put the grated/spiralized apples into a medium-sized bowl.
4. When the sweet potato noodles are cooked, add to the bowl with the apple. Add the egg and cinnamon, and toss until combined.
5. Grease a hot waffle iron with cooking spray. Add 1/4 of the sweet potato noodle mixture and cook for about 4 to 5 minutes or until the waffles are golden brown. Repeat with the remaining sweet potato noodle mixture.
6. Serve immediately, topped with your favorite waffle toppings.

Coconut Biscuits with Crispy Apple Noodles

Prep Time: 10 minutes / Cook Time: 30 minutes

Serves: 8

Preferred spiralizer: Hourglass

Good points: This recipe is high in vitamin B6

Nutritional Information Per Serving: Calories: 190;

Total Fat: 15.4g; Saturated Fat: 9.1g; Trans Fat: 0g;

Cholesterol: 31mg; Sodium: 166mg; Potassium: 237mg;

Total Carbs: 12.6g; Dietary Fiber: 3.3g; Sugar: 7.3g;

Protein: 3.9g; Vitamin A 7%; Calcium: 1%;

Vitamin C: 8%; Iron: 7%

Ingredients:

- ½ cup of soy flour, sifted
- 2 large egg whites
- ½ cup of shredded coconut
- 8 tablespoons of butter
- 2 apples, spiralized
- 7.5 packets stevia
- ¼ teaspoon of salt
- 1 teaspoon of coconut extract
- 2 tablespoons of water
- 1 tablespoon of olive oil

Directions:

1. Preheat the oven to 400 degrees Fahrenheit.
2. In a large bowl, mix the soy flour with the butter, the sugar, the shredded coconut and the salt.
3. In a small bowl, mix the egg whites with the water and the coconut extract.
4. Use a food processor to combine the two mixtures. Blend well until the batter has a rather solid texture.
5. Place a sheet of baking paper over a baking tray and coat it with the olive oil.
6. Using a large spoon, form the cookies and place them in the tray. Bake them for 20-25 minutes.
7. In the meantime, place the apple noodles on another baking tray and drizzle the liquefied butter on them. Place the tray in the oven and cook for 15-20 minutes
8. Remove from the oven and serve the biscuits and the crisp apple noodles after a few minutes in which they cool down.

Apple Barks

Prep Time: 10 minutes / Cook Time: 1 hour

Serves: 24

Preferred spiralizer: Hourglass

Vegetarian-friendly

Good points: This recipe is low in cholesterol and very high in vitamin B6

Nutritional Information Per Serving: Calories: 83;

Total Fat: 4.4g; Saturated Fat: 2.6g; Trans Fat: 0g;

Cholesterol: 3mg; Sodium: 88mg; Potassium: 76mg;

Total Carbs: 9.9g; Dietary Fiber: 1g; Sugar: 8.1g;

Protein: 1.3g; Vitamin A: 0%; Calcium: 2%;

Vitamin C: 2%; Iron: 3%

Ingredients:

- 1 bag (10 ounces) chocolate chips
- 1 1/2 tablespoons almond butter, more as needed
- 2 Honeycrisp apples, medium-sized, spiralized using the Blade C
- 2 tablespoons sliced almonds, more as needed
- 3 teaspoons coconut flakes, more as needed
- Sea salt, to sprinkle (around 1 teaspoon)

Directions:

1. Line an 11x17-inch baking sheet with parchment paper and set aside.
2. Put the chocolate chips in a nonstick pot. Heat over medium heat and stir slowly until the chocolate is melted. Alternatively, you can boil water in a pot, place a glass on the top of the put, put the chocolate chips in the glass, and melt the chocolate, slowly stirring while heating.
3. Pour the melted chocolate into a large-sized bowl. Add the apple noodles and stir well until the noodles break and combine with the chocolate.
4. Pour the chocolate in the prepared baking sheet, spreading in one thin even layer. Evenly top with the almond butter, coconut flakes, almonds and lightly sprinkle with sea salt.
5. Transfer the baking sheet into the freezer and let chill for at least 1 hour or until hard.
6. When hard, slice into 24 squares. Enjoy!

Beet Noodles with Roasted Peaches and Cashews

Prep Time: 10 minutes / Cook Time: 25 minutes

Serves: 6

Preferred spiralizer: Hourglass

Good points: This recipe is very low in cholesterol

Nutritional Information Per Serving: Calories: 175;

Total Fat: 11.8g; Saturated Fat: 4.1g; Trans Fat: 0g;

Cholesterol: 13mg; Sodium: 224mg; Potassium: 289mg;

Total Carbs: 14.2; Dietary Fiber: 2.3g; Sugar: 8.9g;

Protein: 6g; Vitamin A 5%; Calcium: 8%;

Vitamin C: 7%; Iron: 10%

Ingredients:

- 2 cups of beets, spiralized
- 1 cup of peach slices
- ½ cup of cashews, chopped
- ½ cup of Gorgonzola cheese crumbles
- 1 tablespoon of olive oil
- 1 tablespoon of water
- ½ tablespoon of honey
- 1 tablespoon of white balsamic vinegar
- ½ tablespoon of lime juice
- Salt and pepper, to taste

Directions:

1. Preheat your oven to 375F.
2. Set up baking paper on two trays. Cover one tray with the spiralized beets and one with the peach slices. Spray them both with olive oil and season only the beets with salt and pepper.
3. Place the trays in the oven and let them bake for 15-20 minutes.
4. During this time, prepare the dressing. Into a small bowl, combine the water, honey, balsamic vinegar and lime juice. Mix well and season with salt and pepper.
5. When the peaches and beets are cooked, remove them from the tray and add them into a large salad bowl. Pour over the dressing and sprinkle the chopped cashews and cheese crumbles.
6. Toss well and serve.

Spiralized Carrot Cinnamon Dessert

Prep Time: minutes / Cook Time: minutes

Serves: 2

Preferred spiralizer: Hourglass

Vegetarian-friendly

Good points: This recipe has no cholesterol, very low in sodium, high in manganese, and very high in vitamin A.

Nutritional Information Per Serving: Calories: 175;

Total Fat: 14.2g; Saturated Fat: 12.3g; Trans Fat: 0g;

Cholesterol: 0mg; Sodium: 22mg; Potassium: 118 mg;

Total Carbs: 14.4g; Dietary Fiber: 2.6g; Sugar: 10.2g;

Protein: 0.4g; Vitamin A: 102%; Calcium: 5%;

Vitamin C: 3%; Iron: 2%

Ingredients:

- 1 carrot, large-sized, peeled
- 1 tablespoons honey
- 2 tablespoons PLUS 1/4 teaspoon coconut oil
- 2 teaspoons PLUS 1 teaspoon cinnamon
- Tabasco Red Sauce (I used Original)

Directions:

1. Spiralize the carrot. Put 1/4 teaspoon of coconut oil in a pan. Add the carrot and sauté for about 5 minutes over medium heat.
2. While the carrots are cooking, put in the remaining oil, the honey and 2 teaspoons of the cinnamon in a pot. Put in the stovetop and heat over low heat, constantly stirring until the ingredients and the consistency of sauce, about 5 minutes – keep the heat low to avoid boiling or overcooking the sauce and cook continuously stirring. If the honey starts to boil, the honey will get a different flavor and texture.
3. Pour the ready sauce into the skillet with carrots. Keep stirring over medium heat for about 15 minutes and serve warm because the coconut oil will turn solid as it cools.

4. Dash with as much tabasco sauce as desired or sprinkle the top with bananas, raisins, or chia seeds, or whatever you desire.

Notes: This dessert is very sweet so a little amount will cure your sweet tooth desire.

CONCLUSION

Thank you again for downloading this book. I hope that the recipes help you stay on the Low Carb Diet!

Finally, if you enjoyed this book, I'd like to ask you to leave a review for my book on Amazon. It would be greatly appreciated!

Thank you and good luck,

CPSIA information can be obtained
at www.ICGtesting.com
Printed in the USA
BVHW090939210921
617191BV00009B/503